PRAISE FOR *FIX IT, MAKE IT, GROW IT, BAKE IT*

"Let's face it. Life is simple yet somehow most of us complicate it with clutter and wasteful consumerism. This wonderful book helps us get rid of these distractions and focus on the basics."

—Matt Gonzalez, artist, attorney, and environmental activist

"Much more than a how-to guide, *Fix It, Make It, Grow It, Bake It* is a manifesto for living rich while being kind to your pocketbook and planet."

—Nina Lesowitz, co-author of *Living Life as a Thank You* and *The Party Girl Cookbook*

"My copy of *Fix It, Make It, Grow It, Bake It* is filled with highlights, post-its, and dog-ears marking the cool things I want to do. Even a lifelong cheapskate like me learned a lot of ways to live fabulously frugal!"

—Lara Starr, co-author of *The Frugal Foodie Cookbook*

"I love how Billee Sharp weaves together the timeless information (herbs, crafts, gardening, recipes) with the new (freecycling, Wikipedia, open source software)."

—Alicia Bay Laurel, author of *Living on the Earth*

fix it

make it

grow it

bake it

fix it
make it
grow it
bake it

THE DIY GUIDE TO THE GOOD LIFE

BILLEE SHARP

Published in the United States by Viva Editions, an imprint of Cleis Press Inc.,
2246 Sixth St., Berkeley, CA 94710

Printed in the United States.
Cover design: Scott Idleman
Cover illustrations: Eastnine Inc./Getty Images & Frank Wiedemann
Text design and Illustrations: Frank Wiedemann
Cleis logo art: Juana Alicia
First Edition.
10 9 8 7 6 5 4 3 2 1

ISBN: 978-1-57344-365-4

Library of Congress Cataloging-in-Publication Data is available

TABLE OF CONTENTS

FOREWORD

Marriage, motherhood, multiple careers, wise forebears—a stonecutter father, a kitchen-wiz mother, and hardworking, victory-garden-growing grandparents—along with the serious study of sages from J.R.R. Tolkien to Stewart Brand have conferred several lifetimes' worth of wisdom upon Billee Sharp, who can make piñatas, cure cold sores, *and* fix leaky faucets—without spending a dime. Socially aware, eco-conscious citizen that she is, Sharp pays it forward in *Fix It*, a handbook packed with inspiration, ideas, and handy how-tos for every room in the house. From crafting techniques to bath-salt formulas, it's so engagingly written that even the staunchest procrastinator or toolophobe will be coaxed to snatch up shovels, stencils, screwdrivers, and sangria recipes, transforming wardrobes and lifestyles in the process.

Whether you're a diehard DIYer or new to the fold, Billee Sharp is exactly who you want in your (handpainted, rag-rugged, borax-cleansed) corner. As she so eloquently reveals in *Fix It*, she's not only the cheering-squad pal you wish you had; she's also your friendly neighborhood philosopher, career counselor, financial planner, political activist, party organizer, plumber, art instructor, healer, herbalist, beautician, travel agent, decorator, gardener, psychologist, and chef. She describes herself as "a committed daydreamer." But if self-reliance, independence, and the saving of oodles of cash is the result, then the president should appoint a daydreaming czar. I know whom I'd nominate.

Anneli Rufus

INTRODUCTION

Do Your Own Thing!

Most of us are searching for the good life. What constitutes a "good life" is obviously subjective, but our quest to find happiness directs each of our lives in unexpected ways. When I think of personal happiness, security and fulfillment immediately come to mind. We all want the means to realize our hearts' desires, but it is perhaps these desires that need to be reexamined. As a society, we've recently learned the hard way that we often want more than we can afford: our overextended credit system and failed subprime mortgage market have led our economy to a near collapse.

Twenty-first-century life affords us a unique perspective on the world we live in. We are hyperconnected to the rest of the globe, and we are all too aware of the ecological and economic crises that beset contemporary life. We can see that our daily actions have very real repercussions, and what we do as individuals shapes our world both literally and figuratively. We now have an opportunity to take our vision for humanity more seriously.

Slowly, we are acknowledging that the earth does not have the capacity to meet our unrepressed appetites, and that to end the destruction of our environment and the suffering of millions, we have to want less individually.

Our emotional well-being is connected to how much money we have; while it is wretched and distracting not to have enough money to pay the bills, there are also pressures and worries that come with having plenty.

As Duane Elgin notes in his book *Promise Ahead*,

> For many, the American Dream has become the soul's nightmare. Often, the price of affluence is inner alienation and emptiness. Not surprisingly, polls show that a growing number of Americans are seeking lives of greater simplicity as a way to rediscover the life of the soul.

How do we adapt our life expectations accordingly? For me, the desirability of a $7,000 designer handbag evaporates when compared to the number of people that sum could feed. The carbon offsetting system—where individuals calculate their carbon expenditure and try to lower their carbon footprint—is an initiative that shows how seriously we take our situation. Likewise, the growing support for fair-traded goods in commercial markets is evidence that mainstream society is beginning to show more compassion for the people who make and grow our food.

Quite literally, how we see the world has changed. In 1966, with the question "Why haven't we seen a photograph of the whole earth yet?" Stewart Brand initiated a public campaign for NASA to release the satellite image of our planet from outer space. His argument was that the image would be a powerful symbol for humanity, and he was right. Our visualization of the world was changed with our access to this image, and this parallels the dramatic reconfigurations that have transformed Western society. We now have legislation that prohibits discrimination based on color, gender, and religion. Popular opinion and our evolving global consciousness give us hope that humankind can peacefully coexist with one another and with the earth.

I believe that this newly awakened consciousness is due, in large part, to the radical ideas of the Sixties counterculture movement. My own personal philosophy has been shaped by the ideologies of that era, and I felt their impact even as a child. I was impressed by images of student protesters on the evening news and evocative Beatles songs, as well as by an elementary school teacher of mine who wore a purple corduroy suit and a hand-knitted tie and introduced me to *The Hobbit*. I was deeply affected by my elder cousin's vegetarianism and admired the way she and her boyfriend traveled with a guitar so they could make music whenever they wanted it.

I, too, wanted a life of new possibilities. So in the early 1990s I relocated across the globe from London to California, where I started a family and an independent record label with my musician husband. The economic reality of doing our own thing in San Francisco led me to reexamine the ideas of those free-thinking hippies, adopting and adapting as I saw fit. I also started to explore their culture and history in earnest. I began to read Ken Kesey, Jack Kerouac, Tom Wolfe, and Allen Ginsberg, and their mind-blowing literature and poetry led me to radical social theorists like Timothy Leary, Stewart Brand, R. Buckminster Fuller, and Terence McKenna. I also read Alan Watts and Ram Dass on spirituality and Rachel Carson on the environment. I began to see how the cultural revolution that began in the Fifties seeped into all areas of society, from the music and literature of popular culture to the antiwar activism that ended the Vietnam War. I saw its reverberations through the women's movement, the civil rights movement, and environmentalism, and I realized that all these strands are connected through this radical thinking.

The scope of the counterculture movement went beyond theoretical discourse, philosophy, and art into the practical realm of creating a new reality. Alicia Bay Laurel's beautiful manual, *Living On the Earth,* and Stewart Brand's *Whole Earth Catalog* informed a generation about how to live their ideals and rely less on consumer society to survive.

Nor were the counterculturists slow to embrace the communicative power of the Internet. The Well, an early online community that Brand initiated, embodied the principle of interconnectivity that we call "social networking" in today's online world. Futurist thinkers like Buckminster Fuller and Marshall McLuhan believed that technology held the key to social transformation. Fuller characterized our planet as "Spaceship Earth," a miraculous vehicle for which we don't have an operating manual. Fuller considers this a deliberate omission, as we have had to use and develop our intellect to survive. Now, he writes, "We are learning how we can anticipate the consequences of an increasing number of alternative ways of extending our satisfactory survival and growth—both physical and metaphysical."

There is no doubt in my mind that we live in a world enriched by the collective efforts of the flower children, the academics, and the great unsung masses who lived out their ideas and created a new social reality.

For the last 40 years or so, however, society has been looking down upon counterculture, and hippies specifically, applying stereotypes to them such as Birkenstocks, tie-dye, and Dead Heads. The reality is that our culture has been thoroughly enriched by the emphasis of those colorful hippies in community activism, social and political equality, and environmentalism.

Now that we see the cracks in our overcommodified society, more of us are dreaming of finding a simpler life where less is consumed and wasted and where earning the highest income is not our primary goal. We have found that just acquiring and maintaining our wealth has become increasingly onerous and that our individual economies strain under that burden.

Unfortunately, the counterculture visionaries didn't provide us with a foolproof blueprint that we can just superimpose on our 21st-century reality. Some of their concepts, like communal living, no longer seem viable except to a few. Yet while the principles of communal living may not appeal to us now en masse, that spirit is alive and well in grassroots community programs and communal gardens. Cooperatives flourish, too—from food-buying to labor-sharing pools, the hippie ideals live on. The Diggers of San Francisco were a radical street theater group whose activities extended to a Free Bakery, from which they distributed whole wheat loaves made in coffee cans, a Free Store, a Free Clinic, communal living, and art happenings. The Diggers' efforts inspired the Haight-Ashbury Free Clinic, which continues to offer medical treatment to the uninsured, and Food Not Bombs cites the Diggers as an inspiration for their free food program. The counterculture's intoxicating blend of self-discovery and community awareness has enriched our appreciation of the arts and the environment and continues to inspire us to create the culture that we want today. Not surprisingly, the Diggers popularized the expression "Do Your Own Thing!"—and they meant it.

It seems that for a while we shelved those Utopian ideals and began to favor a credit culture in which everything could be acquired now but paid for later. This impractical and irresponsible lifestyle has completely imploded, and although this is a grim reality, I believe the good life we seek does beckon. All we need to do is define it.

On a fundamental level, being committed to friends and family determines the quality of our lives. We are social beings and community is our nourishment—without support we quickly feel vulnerable. It is with humility that we realize that our resources—in all senses—are greater when they are shared.

Our finances are strained in an unstable economy, so we are forced to change our lifestyle accordingly. Now is the time to revive the undervalued virtue of *thrift* and to cut back on the things that we can't afford. This is not a dreary call to economize, but rather an opportunity to scrutinize. What do we really need in order to sustain ourselves?

When we are not weighed down with insurmountable bills, we can pursue the direction of the good life we want. On a practical level, the lower you can make your basic living expenses, the easier they become to meet. Reducing expenses doesn't mean lowering your expectations of a desirable life. In fact, it's quite the opposite. I've found that I get more satisfaction from lower expenditures because I contribute less waste—including product packaging, gas, waste to the landfill, and so on. From this perspective, quite a lot becomes possible.

Joseph Campbell wrote, "Follow your bliss and the universe will open doors where there were only walls." It seems sensible to start by following our passions, which calls to mind the story of Gypsy Boots. Born into a poor immigrant family, Robert Bootzin had an early interest in healthy living; his mother taught him to eat out of the fields and hedgerows. By the time he reached maturity he had evolved into Gypsy Boots, one of the original "Nature Boys" who lived freely off the land in the 1940s. Gypsy Boots and the Nature Boys promoted a healthy vegetarian lifestyle, practiced yoga, and sought to treat all humankind with love and laughter.

In 1958, Gypsy Boots opened Los Angeles's first health food restaurant, the Back to Nature Health Hut, and proceeded to bring his vegetarian ideas to a wider and ultimately influential Hollywood audience. During the Sixties, he became a television personality. He was a regular guest on *The Steve Allen Show*, the perfect platform upon which to spread his ideas even further. *Bare Feet and Good Things to Eat,* his autobiography, detailed his lifestyle ideas and the way he sustained himself and his family by being true to his beliefs. The way Boots describes the management style of his restaurant reminds me of contemporary community kitchen initiatives like the SAME Restaurant in Denver, where guests are requested to pay whatever price they think is fair for their meal; if they don't have enough money, they can pay "in kind" by working in the kitchen.

I'm not suggesting that everybody needs to ditch the SUV and begin a macramé plant-holder business, but I do think that simply doing what makes you happy will reap the best rewards. If you love books, try interning for a publisher to get an insight into their profession, or volunteer at your local library to see how that suits you. In the process you'll surely meet new people, get to share your ideas, and learn a lot about yourself. If you want to stay at home while your kids are young, as I did, find a business you can run from home on your own schedule. My father's advice to my sister and me was to try to make a career out of doing what we loved best—his working life as a stonemason, sculptor, and teacher gave us a good example to follow. He loved stone carving from the first moment he held a chisel in his hand and happily made a good living from his expertise.

My greatest hope is that this book empowers you to think creatively and to create the life that you really want. In this book I offer you suggestions for ways to live happily and affordably while following your dreams and aspirations. I don't have a magic solution or mantra; I am advocating that you reevaluate how you live. Herein you will find all my "trade secrets": tips and tools for how you can live better than ever on less. In working toward creating the good life for my family and friends, I have found much joy, greater peace of mind, and true enjoyment from the simple pleasures in life. I am reminded of the old Native American saying, “Certain things catch your eye, but pursue only those that capture your heart.”

CHAPTER 1

Revolutionary Budgeting: Taking Control of Your Resources

Whatever it is that you really want to do in life, you have the power to make it happen. Over the years, I've developed a plan for making my aspirations come to fruition that requires a new conceptualization of resources and a revision of lifestyle choices. I call this personal economic empowerment *revolutionary budgeting* because it takes a personal revolution for most of us to break out of our consumer-centric reality and think differently about our personal economy. For many, money brings up all our fears and insecurities, but I urge you to shake all that off and step up and take control of your own finances. This act of courage will pay off for the rest of your life.

The foundation steps that I outline here are designed as a guideline for restructuring your strategy toward achieving your vision of the good life you want.

STEP 1: KNOW YOUR GOAL AND PLAN ACCORDINGLY

Figuring out what we want to do with our lives isn't necessarily straightforward and takes some soul-searching. We spend so much of our precious time earning money that it is really important to be able to enjoy our work. To know your path involves tuning out self-doubting fears. You may know exactly what career you want to follow but lack confidence in your direction. Abandon those insecurities and stop listening to the inner curmudgeon who tells you that you don't have the ability or resources to do what you really want to do. There is no useful purpose in doubting yourself. The pertinent issue will be whether you are prepared to do whatever it takes to follow your path: perhaps years of study, with the willingness to downscale your expectations of material wealth.

I feel sad when I hear someone say, "I've always wanted to start a business"—or go to school or become an artist and so on—"but I don't have enough money." I always want to sit them down and have a good chat. I say, do what you love and the money will follow. You just may need to love more than one thing!

This is the situation I've found myself in in recent years: my aim has been to be present in my children's lives and develop as a writer, and these objectives have put a different slant on my work expectations. I have done a lot of interesting and greatly varied work in order to be present for my kids. Likewise, my desire to write has meant that I've needed time to work on my skills and understand the world of publishing—to this end, I interned at a publishing house for six months. In pursuit of realizing my humble dreams, I've worked remotely for an Internet company, done freelance writing, publicity, and marketing, promoted parties and events, baked pies, walked dogs, and started an eco-cleaning service. I wanted to be able to be a full-time mom with a writing habit, and in all these ways I've managed to do exactly that.

Making a major decision about life direction is a huge responsibility and not to be taken lightly. Often, trying something out and getting some preliminary hands-on experience will greatly help you make the right decision. By interning or volunteering, you'll soon find out if you really want to commit.

Ten years ago, I thought I might like to go back to college and earn a law degree. However, I was daunted by the workload and amount of time it would take before I would be eligible to take the bar exam. And the tremendous expense of law school was shocking. I started looking into my options, and I saw that my local community college offered transferable law degree units. These law units also constituted a paralegal qualification, a good backup for me.

I took three law classes and passed them all. I was well on my way to becoming a qualified paralegal, and I also had units that would work as part of a law degree. Suddenly it dawned on me that I would have to work for a corporate law firm for quite a few years to pay off my student loans, which was not at all appealing. Consequently, I stopped the classes. I have always felt good about my decision. I tried it, enjoyed some confidence-boosting success, and, in the process, learned I really did not want to pursue a law career. I was extremely glad that I didn't apply to law school without fully considering the impact it would have on my life. In the process of my studies, while interning at an Eviction Support Center, I learned a huge amount about tenants' rights, which I've subsequently dispensed freely to anybody who has needed advice. I've definitely gained an advantage by having a basic grasp of legal procedures, protocols, and the inside scoop on the baffling legalese that most contracts are written in!

SO WHAT IS IT THAT YOU REALLY WANT TO DO?

If you're not sure about your direction, try this process: write down the jobs that appeal to you, bearing in mind your personal interests— for example, artist, art teacher, art tutor, art therapist, gallerist, curator, art museum worker. All the options following "artist" are art related; whatever your starting point, just keep adding options that seem attractive even if you've never really considered them before. You might have more than one starting point, but you'll create a list of possibilities that you can then research further. Perhaps your friends and the neighborhood kids rave about your cupcakes and you've always dreamed of opening a bakery. Start a little home-based business. If demand rises, you can look into renting a commercial kitchen.

STEP 2: PRACTICE EXTREME THRIFT

Take a long, hard look at your finances. It will be scary for most of us, but be brave—you must establish the bottom line to know what your financial reality is.

Work up a financial budget starting with the basics: figure out your monthly income and your monthly expenses. If your expenses exceed the incoming funds, you must find ways to spend less. Some bills are pretty much fixed, but even mortgages and rents are negotiable, and it is worth trying to get some reduction if your budget is tight.

When my friend Louise had a roommate move out unexpectedly, she needed to save $600 a month. She cut her *New York Times* delivery service and several magazine subscriptions, axed her cable service and her home Internet connection, and reduced her food and wine bills as well. Nobody was more surprised than Louise herself when these few economies covered her shortfall.

When budgeting is tight, it is time to start practicing extreme thrift.

Thrift used to be considered a virtue, and you'll be proud of your self-control when you stop buying anything but essentials. Feel free to take a certain pleasure in having saved even a few dollars; this isn't about being stingy, but rather about appreciating a bargain.

If you have a shortfall between income and expenditures, then it is time to consider reducing your bills and cutting back on some expenses. This doesn't mean that your lifestyle has to suffer; some strategic savings will help you create a budget that will enable you to do what you really want to do. Bills can always be reduced—if you take the time to call and negotiate, you will see where you can save. The initial step is to see if you can reduce your payments while keeping services and insurance policies intact.

The Internet is a valuable resource. As an informational source and as a research tool, it is unrivaled. And while online access does require a computer and an Internet connection, both of which have to be paid for, public libraries have computers and free access.

There are many ways you can save money by doing research online. Certain sites that compare prices of insurance policies, cell phone plans, cable and satellite TV packages, and so on, will make your research easy. You'll find that you can indeed pay less for the same services if you spend the time researching the best prices.

Shopping online will also earn you huge savings on many purchases, undercutting high street prices significantly. Paying bills online saves the cost of stamps and envelopes, with the added bonus of saving trees in the process.

When you're satisfied that you've got the best deals available on your bills but are still over budget, start to consider what you can do without.

Do you really get value from cable TV, or can you live without it? This type of budgetary consideration is very personal—it's about your unique perceptions and needs. But having in mind a baseline budget that you want to achieve is the key, because choosing to cut your expenditures will be easier when your goal is gleaming ahead. It may seem hard to lose familiar comforts, but it is surprising how quickly you can recover. I just let my subscription to *The New Yorker* lapse this year. Although I love it, I don't have time to read it every week. I gathered together all the copies in the house and realized that I'd barely read any of them. I now have a pile of back issues that I'm working through, and when I've read them all, I'll consider subscribing again.

I know a family who decided to axe their cable TV service: they needed to economize and were also concerned with how much time their kids spent viewing. They switched from a $60 monthly service to an online movie service for a third of the price, and everybody was happy. The kids got to order their movies and the parents got to save money and stop worrying about their kids being full time channel-surfing couch potatoes.

Look long and hard at all your monthly expenditures to see what you can do without.

Your quality of life doesn't have to deteriorate because you are spending less money. My friend Sarah refused to consider giving up her membership to a private gym even though she admitted only using the swimming pool and the steam room. She usually only had time to swim a couple of times a week and only managed to get in the steam room a couple of times a month. Eventually, as the gym bill got more difficult to pay, she figured out that she could swim three times weekly at the local public pool and treat herself to a sauna every week and still save $40 a month.

Creating a budget for weekly groceries and household essentials will help you reduce your expenditures. I've found that planning meals keeps my grocery bill in check. I try to plan five evening meals in advance as well as food for a week's breakfasts, lunches, and snacks. In my home, we feed a lot of people in an average week. By buying basic ingredients such as rice, flour, oats, pasta, beans, and legumes in bulk, I always have something in the cupboard to put together a meal without having to make a costly trip to the supermarket. Be as creative as you can with your resources to stay within your budget.

Aside from cutting back on nonessentials and living within your prescribed budget, you should also make a big effort to save. Saving, as I well know, is tough. The three main difficulties I encounter are resisting the temptation to spend, understanding the advantages of saving, and dispelling my optimism that I can make things happen without saving. Save so that you have an emergency fund for unexpected expenses, and set aside a small portion for holidays and gift-giving.

The theoretical advantage of saving is obvious but the interest you earn on savings is the bonus. It is literally free money. Look for high-interest savings accounts that don't have a penalty for the withdrawal of funds. On small amounts, like my holiday savings, the interest won't be huge, but it is still welcome. Larger savings deposits can accrue quite significantly thanks to compound interest. Compound interest is literally "interest on your interest"—it's the bank's way of rewarding you for letting them use your money while you save.

STEP 3: SEEK OUT THE FREE

There are ways to get what you need without spending money, and there are plenty of free resources to tap into. Extreme thrift doesn't mean sacrificing the fun in life—it is there for the taking, and often free. In the Bay Area, where I live, there is a fine tradition of putting unwanted items out on the curb. My place now has a pair of great bookshelves that we found outside a house in the Oakland Hills. Our beloved coffee table is one we spied on the street 15 years ago and have used every day since.

Perhaps the greatest contemporary tool for seeking out the free is the Internet. The free-minded and -spirited have embraced the possibilities of the online world as well as the mercantile one. The gift economy ethos has flourished online with sites like Freecycle (freecycle.org), which operates local networks where participants post their offerings and their needs and keep goods circulating without money being exchanged. The Free section on Craigslist has a few of my friends addicted, and with good reason: one friend acquired an amazing redwood hot tub with a matching wet bar!

There are online resources for free advice on practically anything from legal matters to fixing appliances. There are plenty of free legally downloadable movies and music tracks. Swap-based sites range from book and music trading destinations like Swapmeet.com to Project Gutenberg (gutenberg.org), which offers free ebooks. Shopping online will also bring you huge savings on many purchases, undercutting high street prices significantly.

My favorite free online service has to be free international video phone calls on Skype. Skype offers free downloads of their software, which enables free calls to any computer that has the software installed. After years of not seeing my parents in England regularly, we now can see each other and chat for hours for free.

Free initiatives began before the world went online, but many have utilized the medium. By visiting the website of one of my favorites, the Really Really Free Market, I discovered that there are 27 RRFMs meeting regularly in the States. The RRFM meets once a month, and the market works like a potluck—you bring and take at will. There is absolutely no bartering, trading, or selling; everything is free. Some people bring clothes, bric-a-brac, plants and seedlings, food and drinks, tarot readings, haircuts, legal advice; the list is endless. This kind of initiative is changing ideas about scarcity and revitalizing our ability to simply share. If there isn't an RRFM in your area, visit their website (www.reallyreallyfree.org) and get tips on how to start one.

In our community, we are blessed to have a fabulous weekly Free Farm Stand, which offers free locally grown produce to all comers, as well as seedlings and gardening advice. We are witnessing a huge growth in community gardening initiatives, where people are coming together to grow food in their gardens and reclaimed lots. The free scene vibe is that scarcity does not really exist in our society and that sharing our surplus makes complete sense. SF Glean (sfglean.org), another great local example, is a nonprofit that harvests fruits and nuts from local garden trees and donates it to food banks, homeless shelters, and the Free Farm Stand. Produce To The People runs a similar harvesting program in the same small city, which just goes to show how much food is being grown that people are willing to share. If you research your area and don't find this kind of initiative, it might be time to start one up yourself.

Freeganism is a philosophy and a practice of utilizing the free abundance around us. Freegans, in their own words, "employ alternative strategies for living based on limited participation in the conventional economy and minimal consumption of resources." They are famous for dumpster diving for food and other goods and embracing the concept of cooperation. The official Freegan website (freegan.info) makes for fascinating reading and lists all existing Freegan networks worldwide as well as offering tips for the lone dumpster diver.

HOW TO SAVE

- Keep a change jar. When it's full, put the money in your savings account.
- Save a dollar a day.
- Research online savings accounts—they have the best interest rates.
- Set realistic goals for saving. Save what you can afford.
- Start an automatic savings plan with your bank.
- Use your credit card to make purchases, pay the card in full every month, and earn cash and travel credits.
- Avoid ATM fees. Only withdraw from machines approved by your bank for free use.
- Buy your checks from a check company; they are much cheaper than the bank.
- Get paid to be environmentally friendly. You can make an offer on all electronic equipment at gazelle.com. They pay for shipping and even send you a box!

STEP 4: SELL, TRADE, AND BARTER

The fourth step is to take a good look at all your possessions and see what you don't need that you can sell. Yard sales and Internet selling sites such as eBay and Craigslist can make you money with a little effort. This is a good way to kick-start a savings plan or to supplement your deposits. It really is money for old rope and another way to keep serviceable stuff out of the landfill. If you keep a record of how much you make, you'll be encouraged. Organizing can be onerous, but it's amazing how much unwanted stuff you'll find when you start opening the cupboards. Doing a yard sale can be fun—even the kids like to have a little pitch! When we do a yard sale we generally invite friends to join us in selling. A large collection of bric-a-brac draws more attention, and hanging out with friends all day is a bonus. Try posting on local online bulletin boards or running a little ad in your local paper. List your most tantalizing offerings, and you'll get early visitors. How you set up your yard sale will affect your sales; remember to make things accessible—its worth pulling out some tables to display items on. Clothes look better on hangers, and shoes look better clean and in pairs.

When my husband, Jonah, is trying to figure out how he can afford a new piece of electronic music equipment, he culls his existing collection to create the funds. Many times I've questioned what he has decided to sell, but he is strict with himself: if he doesn't use something regularly and it is replaceable if he should have a need for it in the future, he has no compunction about letting the item go.

You should consider selling anything that you don't use regularly and that has a monetary value. Creating an area to store outgoing items for sale, trade, or giving away free will stimulate the process. If you are advertising online, you should take photos of your salable items. Find a spot that works well for photographing and designate it as your studio.

Trading your skills, labor, or possessions is another resource. Trading doesn't lead to hard cash but is an excellent way to enhance your budget. I've traded childcare and tutoring for childcare and tutoring, enabling me to have both a social life and a respite from algebra, which I still don't entirely understand!

There are infinite possibilities for trading skills; anything you can do that might appeal to potential trading partners will work. We traded two weeks' use of our home entertainment system for two weeks in a glamorous four-room tent with air beds. So, in exchange for services rendered, we got a memory that will last a lifetime.

Some tradable activities can also be realized as side jobs where you are working for cash. Our friend Chloe was running her own independent record label but wasn't making quite enough, so she started trading her consummate clothes ironing skills for help building her website. Word spread quickly about her immaculately pressed shirts. Her ironing prowess proved to be much in demand and lucrative; she ironed a couple of hours a day and made extra money. This would be some people's idea of hell, but she found it calming and meditative—it takes all sorts. Getting the word out that you are available for such activities will bring opportunities. Try sending an e-mail to likely contacts explaining what you can offer and asking what they might trade back. I generally figure out what I need and whom I could ask, and then I think about what might be appealing to those people. When I needed help with my taxes one year and couldn't afford it, I asked a tax consultant friend if she could help me. Because I knew she was always busy with paperwork, I offered to trade clerical work. She snapped up my offer, and I spent an afternoon envelope-stuffing for her while she reviewed my tax return.

Defining your personal economy is empowering: instead of feeling that some things are beyond your financial reach, get creative about procuring what you need. I believe it's liberating to be able to "pay" without using money. It certainly engenders a different value system and an economically valid mode of exchange. The idea that there is a definitive "price" does not figure in the trading model. The trade is mutually beneficial and doesn't have to have an equivalent fiscal value; it just has to work for the traders.

STEP 5: ECO-ECONOMY

In the process of refining your revolutionary budget, consider your choices in terms of ecological impact. Try to use less to live better; you will find that saving the planet saves you money, too. Holding back from new purchases and reusing existing stuff reduces landfill. Fixing broken stuff is equally desirable, and if you can't fix it, offer it to others before throwing it away. When I first joined Freecycle.org I was amazed at how much broken stuff was advertised on the list, but pleasantly surprised to see how the broken stuff finds new homes, too. Every time we go to buy something, we need to consider the environment. The less packaging our food comes in, the less we contribute to the plastic contamination of the planet. The smallest gestures are worthwhile, because the choices we make about the way we live will affect our global reality. Think about respecting the earth by choosing to walk to the store instead of driving, switch off lights religiously, and unplug appliances when they're not in use.

My family's electricity bill became a problem at one point. My husband has a music studio in our basement, and most of his equipment plugs in and functions best when it doesn't get switched off, ever. This led to high electricity bills that became a monthly burden. Because the studio is the basis of our livelihood, we couldn't just power down every day and risk the potential malfunctioning of his rig, which in turn leads to loss of revenue. One day, our clothes dryer broke down. It was during the summer, so I started to hang the wash out in the back garden on a makeshift line. Our next electricity bill was down by 20 percent, and consequently we never replaced the dryer. At first I thought it would be a lot of extra work, but the savings have been worth the effort. I really enjoy hanging out the wash, and it also gives me a chance to be in the garden. In the winter, when the sun is hiding and the backyard clothesline is less effective, our kitchen chairs and doors get draped with drying clothes. The savings we have made by doing without a clothes dryer have offset the cost of running the studio. In a pinch, I'll go down to the Laundromat to dry clothes—an occasional inconvenience I'm happy to live with.

That 20 percent saving is much enhanced by the sense of satisfaction that I get from knowing that I am not only saving money but also helping the environment (albeit in a tiny way). The monthly savings aggregate to an annual saving of $240, and now that I have the electricity-saving bug, I'm always conserving electricity wherever I can and checking my bills to see the impact of my vigilance.

A few years ago I decided to start a small business so that I could work to my own schedule and have my livelihood reflect my environmental concerns. I had been cleaning my home with environmentally friendly products for years and realized that this was something I could turn into a business. The legal start-up costs for a small business are not large. Registering your business name and procuring a license from your local authority are the only things you need to take care of. I took out a housecleaning insurance policy to cover my work practice, which is standard procedure in the housecleaning business.

Once I was authorized to do the work, I only had to furnish myself with the tools of the trade and look for jobs.

A cleaning service is a good example of a low-capital start-up business. I needed only a vacuum cleaner, a broom, a mop, a few scrubbing tools, rags for cleaning and buffing (which I made out of old towels and T-shirts), and cleaning products. The vacuum cleaner and broom I already had, and the cleaning products I made myself, using cheap and effective ingredients like baking soda, vinegar, borax, Castile soap, and essential oils. (Find cleaning recipes for your home or cleaning business in Chapter 4, Homely Habitats.)

These simple steps helped me build a business without spending very much money at all. Word-of-mouth referrals from friends and posting my services online got the business up and running. Apart from the business being easy and affordable to set up and run, I got immense satisfaction from knowing that I was propagating environmentally friendly practices in homes and workplaces.

CHAPTER 2

Health Is Wealth

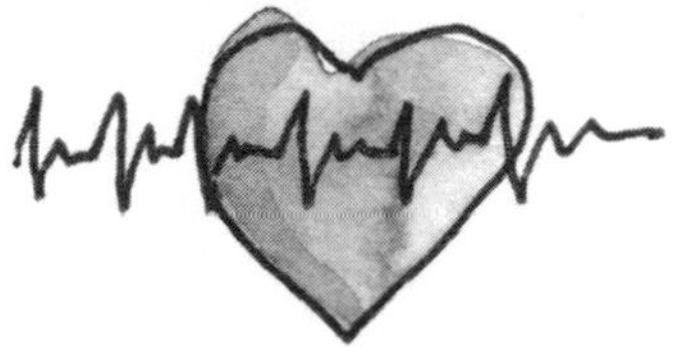

Our health is the foundation of our wealth. To achieve the good life, we have to be able to function at our best, and good health is the key. Our diet has to be our first consideration, because when we are well fed, we function better both emotionally and physically. You can eat to support your well-being without spending a fortune, but chances are, certain aspects of your lifestyle are going to have to change. The idea is to optimize nutrition with the food choices we make, thereby reducing our expenditures and increasing our health.

I remember when a neighborhood boy who was playing at our house opened our fridge and exclaimed, "There's nothing in here!" My 5-year-old son was really embarrassed, but I took the time to explain to our small visitor that our fridge just looked empty to him, but there actually was a lot of food in there waiting to be eaten. I showed him the ingredients for a couple of meals I had planned, as well as the snacks I could easily conjure up, too. What threw the little guy off was an absence of prepared and packaged foods, juice boxes, yogurt containers, packs of individual string cheese, and so on. There was plenty there; he just wasn't used to seeing it "in the raw," so to speak.

Even when it seems there is nothing in the house to eat, our cupboards are generally full. I recommend doing a "kitchen inventory" where you literally take stock. Pulling everything out of the cupboards and onto the kitchen table and sifting through our supplies can be quite revealing and will probably yield a few meals. When the crumbs have been swept away, we can restock with basics.

Although it's easier to use prepared and processed foods, this is substantially more expensive than basic ingredients and usually offers less nutrition. Cooking, baking, sprouting, and fermenting are foreign territory to many of us, but we can ease into a lifestyle where these skills can be learned and even enjoyed.

New Food Reality! The quickest way to a healthy, affordable diet is to eat at home. By this, I don't mean heating up prepared foods. Prepared foods generally contain undesirable ingredients like hydrogenated oils, refined sugars, refined grains, artificial sweeteners, high-fructose corn syrup, and too much salt! The nutritive value of these additives is negligible but the detrimental effects are significant, especially to heart health. Refined sugars and grains constitute "bad" cholesterol, as do hydrogenated oils. It is "bad" cholesterol that leads to risk of heart disease, heart attacks, and strokes. Always check the ingredient lists of prepared foods. Ingredients are listed in order of priority; the higher up the list, the more there is of an ingredient in the food.

Buying basic foodstuffs and making meals from scratch will greatly reduce your grocery bills. When you are no longer buying expensive prepared foods, you can use the extra savings to buy the best-quality basics.

My definition of *basics* is the essential ingredients that you need to make great, healthy food: grains, flours, legumes, pastas, fresh and dried fruits and vegetables, fats, oils, protein, and seasonings. A huge variety of recipes can be made from a solid base of these food groups. The way to start is to keep it simple. Don't start with cheese sauce—go with a stir-fry and make easy dishes that don't take a lot of culinary know-how. Remember, simpler is better and healthier.

WHAT'S THE DIFFERENCE?

Buying organic and fair-traded foods is the best option, for both nutritive and ethical value. Organic and fair-traded basic foods will invariably cost the most, but the difference in price between organic and fair-traded organic is often only a matter of cents. Organic status for foods and produce in the United States is certified by the USDA National Organic program. The term *fair-traded* is applied to goods that have been monitored to ensure fair prices and fair labor conditions. Fair-traded goods are sourced by direct trade from the producers, which encourages community development and a strict adherence to environmentally sustainable practices. If paying a few cents extra works for your budget, you can enjoy the ethical value of fair-traded goods, but if you are on a strict budget, buy plain organic. If the budget is especially tight—conventionally grown it is! I try not to be overzealous about always buying organic. I can't always afford it, so I take advantage of special offers and remember that bulk is most often significantly cheaper by weight than packaged goods.

In Chapter 6, Eat, Drink, and Be Merry, I guide you through a complete revamping and restocking of your kitchen and show you recipes for delicious meals, snacks, and treats that are easy and affordable.

If you feel that your kitchen is full of stuff you'll never use, get it all out of the cupboards and be ruthless. Canned and preserved foods that are still edible

should be considered for an emergency kit, but not if it's stuff that you don't like! Give all undesired foods to a food bank or a shelter; it doesn't need to go to waste.

POSITIVE PACK RAT

- Keep glass jars and bottles; you can use them to store items bought in bulk. Save pretty jars and bottles for making tinctures, cordials, bath salts, and so on.
- Keep plastic containers with fitted lids for storing leftovers in the fridge; use them for starting plants by perforating the bottoms for drainage.
- Buy as much as you can in bulk, and decant quantities into smaller containers for everyday use.
- Don't buy plastic bags: keep plastic bags from the market and use them to store veggies or open dishes in your fridge. Reuse plastic bags to line wastebins, pick up pet droppings, and other uses that don't require a clean bag.

EATING FOR THE ENVIRONMENT

- Cutting back on meat consumption is good for the environment, your health, and your wallet. Designate one day a week "meat free" and know that you are helping reduce greenhouse gas emissions. To produce one pound of beef puts as much carbon dioxide into the environment as driving a typical car 70 miles!
- Read "Livestock's Long Shadow," the 2006 UN paper on the effects of the meat industry on the environment and human populations: www.fao.org/docrep/010/a0701e/a0701e00.HTM.
- Sir Paul McCartney and many other celebrities support Meat Free Mondays. Check it out at www.meatfreemondays.co.uk. The Belgian city of Ghent has instituted a Meat Free Thursday. Get inspired and start a local meat-free day!
- Start a farm-to-school project in your school district; all the know-how is at www.farmtoschool.org.

DON'T PANIC: GO ORGANIC

We need to look at the level of contamination in our diet: the food industry has, perhaps unwittingly, used the human race as a beta test, trying out all sorts of innovations in food production. Pesticides and genetically modified organisms, or GMOs, together with farming and animal husbandry methodologies, have changed the quality of our food dramatically in the last hundred years. The ramifications are still largely unknown, but as John Robbins, author of *Diet for a New America* and *The Food Revolution*, says, "the chemical industry has mounted an aggressive campaign to discredit organic food. And without the knowledge or consent of most Americans, two-thirds of the products on our supermarket shelves now contain genetically engineered ingredients."

The debate is ongoing, but organic foodstuffs produced with a minimum of chemical interference rank higher nutritionally, as attested by a recent paper in the *State of Science Review* by the Organic Center in cooperation with Washington State University, titled "New Evidence Confirms the Nutritional Superiority of Plant-Based Organic Foods." Most processed food has a significant number of ingredients that are superfluous to the inherent nutritive value—preservatives and artificial coloring come quickly to mind. A revealing study in *Middleton's Allergy Principles and Practice* documents research into the phenomenal rise in allergies, which have a direct correlation to the volume of contaminants in our food and environment.

We also have to consider our ethical accounting—trying to support our desire for global change on an individual level. When we buy organic and unprocessed foods, we are supporting the market for these products. To reduce our individual impact on global warming, we try to support local producers, thereby bringing down the carbon footprint of our vittles. The 2006 United

Nations report "Livestock's Long Shadow" on the impact of meat production is alarming: "[the meat industry is] one of the top two or three most significant contributors to the most serious environmental problems, at every scale from local to global." A vegan diet has a high ethical value as well as health benefits, but our carnivorous nature is hard to reprogram. Eating meat only a couple of times a week goes a long way to help. Calculate your environmental footprint at www.myfootprint.org, and perhaps you'll decide to cut back on your meat and poultry consumption. Likewise, carrying out coffee from home rather than succumbing to the ubiquitous latte will save you money as well as a lot of paper cups and plastic lids that are likely to go directly into the landfill.

Ultimately, our power as consumers will have a direct effect on what is available to us and how much it costs, so vote with your purse and buy ethically. If this sounds like a great idea in theory but financially out of reach for you, then you have to do the math: if you buy basics in bulk, the price difference between most organic (even fair-traded) and conventional items is marginal. Many whole-food stores have discount days to support their customers' budgets. the Rainbow Cooperative store in San Francisco offers coupons for two 20 percent off days every week. We reduce the packaging load when we buy bulk, reuse plastic bags, and take a basket to the farmer's market.

We need to educate ourselves about the way we buy food and consider how we eat. The variables are time and mindfulness. I'm advocating for the course that takes more time and asks for more consideration. I know it takes longer to prepare a meal from scratch than just heating up a prepared packaged dish, but the payoffs—good health, family, community, and simple enjoyment—are absolutely worth it. I try to cook enough for two meals at a time so that we have leftovers for lunches, latecomers, and snacks.

In some systems of belief, this mindful attention to our food and how we prepare it is an important part of eating well. In the Ayurvedic tradition, the practice of careful preparation—giving a loving energy to making a meal—makes it good to eat. When you feed people with food that you have planned out, shopped for, prepared, and served, your devotion is apparent and always appreciated.

May your food be your medicine and your medicine be your food.

—Hippocrates

SOLAR OVENS

Solar ovens are inexpensive to buy, easy to use, and you'll cook for free every time you use one. Solar ovens cook food without using electricity, fossil fuels, or propane. Food cooked in a solar oven retains all vitamins and minerals. Solar ovens also pasteurize water for drinking. A solar oven is perfect for your emergency supply kit.

Check out www.solarovens.org to see the great work this nonprofit is doing with solar ovens in Third World countries.

THE HEALTHY PANTRY

PLASTIC CONTAINERS

Bulk items need to be stored. The clear plastic bags they arrive in from the store will suffice, but large glass jars and airtight containers are much better for purposes of organization and labeling. It is also worth noting the emerging health concerns around the safety of plastic food and drink containers. Research has shown that some grades of plastics leach chemicals into the foods or liquids stored in them. Disposable soda and water bottles shouldn't be reused, because through general wear and tear and exposure to heat they leach Bisphenol A, a hormone-disrupting chemical. Lexan plastic (polycarbonate plastic), the type of hard plastic often used for reusable drink bottles, also leaches Bisphenol A. Baby bottles used to be made of polycarbonate plastic, but, thankfully, these are no longer manufactured. Plastics graded #1 (PET/PETE), #3 (PVC) and #6 (polystyrene/PS) have all been shown to leach chemicals into foods or liquids. For this reason, I believe it's preferable to use stainless steel or glass containers. Make sure that you don't buy a stainless-steel bottle with a plastic lining. Glass jars filled with bulk grains, teas, and spices can be quite pretty, with the added plus that it is healthier for your family.

KITCHEN ESSENTIALS

You may find that you don't actually need the three blenders, two toasters, and various coffeemakers that have been proliferating in your cupboards. Sell, barter, and trade these items, and add to your savings. Don't keep too much stuff, because now that you are going to be cooking more than ever, you'll need room to store the goods and utensils that you'll be using all the time and more counter space to actually prepare your food.

My list of kitchen essentials consists of the absolute basics: a chopping board, a chopping knife, two or three cooking pots of various sizes (I have a 1-quart pot and two medium saucepans) a big skillet, a small skillet, a grater, a colander, a few wooden spoons, cookie sheets, and a couple of spatulas—that's it! Since we have a Pizza Friday ritual, we have a pizza stone. This can be used for baking bread as well, or you can bake the loaves in a skillet. Salad spinners, juicers, blenders, and bread machines are great assets, but you can get started without them and, as in my case, manage pretty well for many years.

DETOX YOUR DIET

Overhauling your eating habits is a major undertaking—it's a detox in itself. There are always viable reasons for a detox, and a simple program is easy and free. The idea is to cleanse yourself internally, and a diet as simple as rice and lentils or rice and steamed vegetables is a gentle way to do it. Drink only water and herbal teas with this reduced diet, and keep with it for three days. In the macrobiotic tradition, bancha twig tea is used to support the cleanse, but nettle, peppermint, or another herbal tea that you like is fine. This kind of detox diet will make you feel good, but you won't be wiped out in the process. You should discuss juice diets, fasts, and other hard-core cleanses with your physician or a nutritionist, and you'll need to have an open schedule to commit to this kind of cleanse, as the physical effects can include light-headedness and weakness.

When you are ready to start reintegrating solid foods into your diet, do so slowly and see how you feel. Try not to dive back into white flour and white sugar products; use this time to initiate the dietary changes that you've planned.

SKIN DETOX

Dry or wet skin brushing is a good therapy to enhance a detox diet. Buying a brush is the only expenditure, but there is an alternative that a friend of mine introduced me to. She gave me a little hand-sewn glove made of a textured crepe de Chine fabric, which works exactly the same way, wet or dry: applied with a circular motion to the skin. This is something you could just sew yourself—any textured fabric would work to stimulate the skin.

A home facial is easy to do and will help your skin release dirt and impurities trapped by your pores. Simply boil water and transfer it to a medium-size bowl. Add a drop of your favorite essential oil, and place a towel over your head to create a "tent" over the bowl of hot water. Use a large enough towel that you can drape it over you and the bowl without hot air escaping, and stay under it as long as you are comfortable. When you have finished steaming, splash your face with cold water to close your clean and refreshed skin pores.

SEA SALT SCRUB

Sea salt makes an invigorating exfoliating skin rub, which will help you detox, and is best used in the shower, where you can rinse off easily afterward. Sea salt should be among your kitchen basics, and you can use it for both personal and housecleaning needs, as well as for cooking.

I remember the first time I used a sea salt scrub; it was a gift from a friend, and I loved it. My skin felt amazingly smooth and hydrated, and I promised myself that I would treat myself to it again.

The store-bought item was too pricey for me, but then I found an easy recipe for making my own. The ingredients are all very affordable, and the method is simple enough. Your friends will love this as a gift, and the home-made scrub will last indefinitely in a closed container. Use interesting glass jars—colored glass works nicely—and tie on a scrap of recycled ribbon to make a luxurious but inexpensive present.

SCRUMPTIOUS SKIN SCRUB

coarse sea salt

base oil: any one or a combination of canola, safflower, almond, sesame, apricot kernel, avocado, jojoba

essential oil: your favorite or a combination of lavender, rose, geranium, lemon, peppermint, thyme, ginger, mint

Fill a quart jar or other lidded container about three-quarters with sea salt.

Infuse a cup of base oil with 10–15 drops of essential oil, and pour it over the sea salt, covering the salt by at least an inch. Stir, and leave it to set. You can seal your container as soon as the ingredients have been added.

If you have fresh lavender or rosemary growing nearby, snip a few twigs and tie them to your jar with ribbon.

Some people like their scrubs more oily than others. Adjust the amount of essential oil you use to your own preference. When using the scrub, remember to rub vigorously, working from your extremities toward your heart to enhance your circulation. Rub your elbows and knees with a circular motion. Exfoliate, rinse, and relax!

THE DETOX BATH

Epsom salts, made from the mineral magnesium sulfate, are a great therapeutic addition to a bath. When a spring with magnesium sulfate deposits was discovered in the small town of Epsom in Surrey, England, the salts got their name. When Epsom salts are absorbed by the skin, they relax strained muscles, draw toxins from the body, sedate the nervous system, and reduce swelling. They also exfoliate old, dry skin and soften hard, calloused skin. Two cups of salts in a hot bath with a few drops of your favorite essential oil is luxurious, but this recipe is my ultimate detox bath:

SEA SALT BATH

1 cup each coarse sea salt, Epsom salts, and baking soda

1–2 tablespoons glycerin, to keep your skin from drying

3–5 drops essential oil

Stir together, add half to running bath, and add the rest when the bath is drawn. This mixture will keep indefinitely in a closed container.

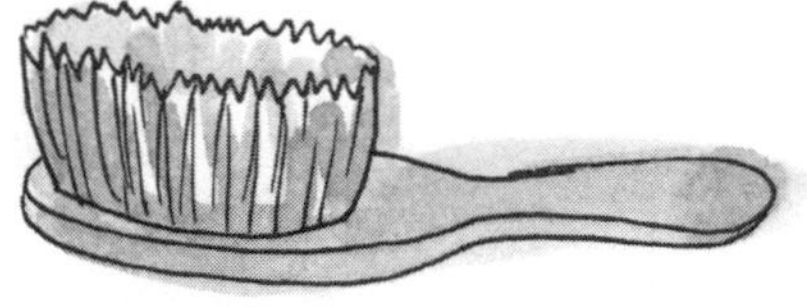

BARBARA'S PRISON WORKOUT

You don't have to go to the gym to get fit and toned. Here is the daily regimen that my friend Barbara devised for us when we decided to battle the bulge. It's easy to get in shape without spending money on personal trainers and gym memberships. This workout can be realized in your living room!

Push-ups: 3 sets of 10

Tricep dips: 3 sets of 10

Sit-ups: 3 sets of 10

Bicep curls: 3 sets of 10

Holding plank: 3 minutes straight

Hindu squats: 25–50 in repetition

DAILY YOGA

Check out free yoga classes and look for introductory rates at yoga studios. You can study online to learn asanas, too—there are many sites, often with videos. I do the Moon Salutation three times a day to tone my body and mind. The Moon Salutation was developed in the 1980s as a sequence of movements calming to the nervous system and supportive of women through menstruation, pregnancy, and menopause. Men love the Moon Salutation too! Check out the Moon here: http://www.lauracornell.com/moon/html.

Or try the Sun Salutation. There is a great instructional video here: http://www.metacafe.com/watch/351572/sun_salutation_instructions/.

Start a daily practice with the Moon or Sun Salutation, and spend a few minutes meditating to improve your energy and serenity!

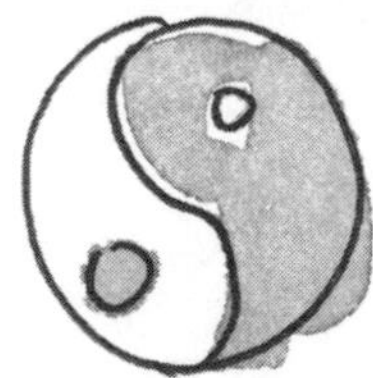

KITCHEN CABINET CURES

It's great to be able to treat your family's ailments at home without having to take off for the doctor's office. Of course, if you feel there is cause for serious concern, a doctor's visit is a must. However, there are plenty of powerful curative and preventive remedies available that you can stock at home at very little expense. Today, with the cost of health care skyrocketing, healthy home remedies are a smart option to add to your family's regimen.

I keep a good selection of herbal teas for everyday drinking and for use as remedies. I also keep several teapots and designated mason jars on hand for steeping tea. If you are using an herbal tea as a curative, it's a good idea to steep it overnight so the tea is stronger—then you can add hot water to dilute to your taste. Nettle tea steeped overnight becomes a brilliant dark green, and subtle flavors like red raspberry leaf teas become more defined.

HERBAL TEAS

The basic teas listed below sustain my household, and herbal tea is an easy way into learning herb lore. This introduction may lead you to discover the herbs that are most useful and beneficial to you and your family.

Peppermint (tummy upset, digestive tonic)
Nettle (blood cleansing, antihistamine, great source of iron)
Sage (cleansing, sore throats, night sweats)
Chamomile (calming)
Oatstraw (calms nervous energy, great source of calcium)
Red raspberry leaf (reproductive health tonic)
Blackberry (like red raspberry, also good for coughs, colds, and diarrhea)
Thyme (coughs, bronchitis)

Herbal tinctures, which are concentrated reductions of the herbs, are more expensive but last longer and provide a higher dose of the herb. We keep a tincture of Echinacea and goldenseal in the house year round. At the first sign of a cold or cough, a few drops go into herbal teas and hot lemon and honey toddies. A hot toddy is traditionally made with hot water, lemon, sugar or honey, and a liquor such as brandy, but it doesn't have to be alcoholic to be medicinal. Fresh ginger and garlic are great for adding to home remedies, particularly for colds; just chop finely or grate and add to teas and toddies.

HERBAL DECOCTIONS

To make a tea from the root, bark, or stems of plants you will need to make a decoction: add approximately 2 tablespoons of the herb to 1 cup of water and gently simmer for half an hour.

GINGER CURATIVES

Ginger is indicated for a sore throat and is a good addition to a hot toddy for cold symptoms. Ginger is known to alleviate indigestion, general nausea, upset tummy, morning sickness, motion sickness, and stomach flu. Ginger tea has a very pleasant taste, and you can buy tea bags or gently boil slices of fresh ginger root to make the tea yourself; I recommend using the fresh ginger root for maximum taste and potency. Arthritic pain can be treated with ginger, too; 3–4 grams (about 1⁄10 of an ounce) daily is recommended, and ground ginger can be used in capsules, or tincture of ginger.

RECOVERY AID

When you are getting over an illness, eat light broths: vegetable, chicken, or meat. Broths are easy to digest, saving your body's energy for recovery.

GARLIC POWER

Garlic is well known for its protection against infection and should be used regularly, to taste, in your cooking. It is also known to reduce cholesterol levels and can be helpful in lowering blood pressure. Rich in vitamins A, B, and C, garlic is an excellent source of minerals: selenium, iodine, potassium, iron, calcium, zinc, and magnesium. The active component in garlic is allicin, a sulfur compound produced when garlic is chopped, chewed, or bruised. It is powerful as an antibiotic and helps the body inhibit the ability of germs to grow and reproduce. When preparing garlic, cut or crush the cloves and let the garlic rest for 10 minutes before cooking or eating to allow the allicin to develop. Garlic is cited as therapeutic for the treatment of many health conditions, such as high and low blood pressure, heart health, and asthma, as well as being acknowledged as an anticancer agent and preventive for colds and other infections.

Although garlic pills are available, raw garlic is just as effective and considerably cheaper. For a simple garlic tonic to guard against colds or just to boost your general health, crush a couple of cloves and add a tablespoon of olive oil. Taking a spoonful of garlic in olive oil works well if you don't like the taste or are fearful of unappealing, garlicky breath.

At the onset of an earache, take a peeled clove, wrap it in a little fabric, and stick it in your sore ear. Leave it there overnight, and you will feel some relief by the morning.

GRAPEFRUIT SEED EXTRACT

Grapefruit seed extract is a powerful substance. It is very strong and should never be taken undiluted or used neat in a topical application. I use it when afflicted with a stomach bug with symptoms of vomiting and diarrhea. Take 5–10 drops in 8 ounces of juice or tea, which will help disguise its strong, bitter taste. For a child, give 3–5 drops in 5 ounces of juice or tea. These doses should be taken morning and evening, and will clear up a stomach bug pretty quickly. After taking grapefruit seed extract, also take some acidophilus, either in a natural yogurt or tablet form. This will restore your "friendly" intestinal flora to a healthy, balanced state. Grapefruit seed extract is also recommended as a gingivitis treatment: add 3 drops to 5 ounces of water and use as a mouthwash—rinse and spit, but try not to swallow!

For an effective dandruff cure, add 5 drops to your usual dollop of hair shampoo and massage it into the scalp.

For a wart or cyst, apply a drop of grapefruit seed extract daily directly to the affected spot and cover with a bandage.

ALOE VERA JUICE AND GEL

As a topical application, aloe vera gel is great for all kinds of burns, including sunburn. It has been shown to have therapeutic value in the healing of skin lesions caused by psoriasis. The juice is a great general tonic recommended as an aid to digestion, a stimulus for intestinal health, and a gentle colon cleanse. Aloe vera is one of the few vegetarian sources of vitamin B12, containing 19 amino acids, 20 minerals, and 12 vitamins, all having a beneficial effect on general health. Drinking 4 to 8 ounces daily diluted in juice or taken neat is recommended, but just a couple of times a week will be beneficial.

BAKING SODA BENEFITS

Baking soda is great in a bath if your skin is irritated, especially for poison oak, as the soda will help dry up wet blisters as well as greatly reducing the itch. Applying a baking soda and water paste to the site of a bee sting or other insect bites will neutralize the pain and itch. Just remove the actual sting first, and smooth on the baking soda paste for instant relief.

A headache can be treated with a teaspoon of baking soda dissolved in a cup of warm water with ¼ cup of freshly squeezed lemon juice.

Last but not least, whiten your teeth by brushing with baking soda and water.

WITCH HAZEL WISDOM

Witch hazel is an excellent and inexpensive astringent and antiseptic to always keep on hand. Topical uses for witch hazel include cleaning cuts, reducing skin inflammations and abrasions, sunburn, insect bites, bruising, poison oak and ivy, diaper rash, eczema, varicose veins, and hemorrhoids.

Preparations of witch hazel from the pharmacy generally contain isopropyl alcohol, so make sure you only use it externally, as it is poisonous to ingest. Make cold compresses with witch hazel for painful hemorrhoids, varicose veins, or other skin inflammation and bruises. For a witch hazel tincture, add 15 drops to a small bowl of warm water, immerse a clean washcloth in the solution, and leave it soaking for 5 minutes. Wring out the washcloth and lay it on the affected area.

As an astringent, witch hazel works well for drying sores, diaper rash, and poison oak and ivy. Use witch hazel tincture (5 drops to 8 ounces of water) if you want to avoid the isopropyl alcohol.

ESSENTIAL OILS FOR HEALTH

Essential oils have been used medicinally for centuries. They are extracted from flowers, grasses, shrubs, herbs, and trees. If you are skeptical about the efficacy of essential oils, you'll at least find it reassuring to know that the oils enter and exit the human body without leaving any toxins behind. The best ways to use essential oils are externally, absorbed through the skin, or through steam inhalation. However, oral applications are indicated for some remedies.

There are hundreds of essential oils used by herbalists, but for general therapeutic use in the home, these are my recommendations.

LAVENDER OIL

If I could only have one essential oil, I would choose lavender because it is so versatile. It is a natural antibiotic, antiseptic, sedative, antidepressant, topical treatment for scalds and burns, a good detoxifier, prevents scarring, promotes healing, and its lovely scent has a calming effect and is widely used in aromatherapy.

TEA TREE OIL

Used by aborigines in Australia for centuries, tea tree oil is a powerful antibacterial, antifungal, and antiseptic. It has a fresh camphor smell and is used to treat athlete's foot, sunburn, candida, and other infections.

PEPPERMINT OIL

A wonderful therapeutic for digestive, respiratory, and circulatory complaints, peppermint oil is used to treat indigestion, irritable bowel syndrome, flatulence, halitosis, catarrh, varicose veins, headaches, skin irritations, and rheumatism. It also works as a deterrent for infestations of mice, fleas, and ants. It is not surprising that peppermint oil is regarded as the world's oldest medicine.

EUCALYPTUS OIL

In eucalyptus oil we have an all-purpose antiviral, antibiotic, diuretic, analgesic, and antiseptic. It can be therapeutic for coughs, colds, respiratory stimulation, and insect bites. If you start to feel cold symptoms, use 5 drops of eucalyptus oil in a hot bath or in a bowl prepared with boiling water for a head steam.

THYME OIL

Thyme is an "old-time" antiviral, antibiotic, antiseptic, and diuretic curative; it was highly valued and widely used by the ancient Egyptians, Greeks, and Romans for fatigue, coughs, warts, rheumatism, neuralgia, and acne. Thyme oil works very well mixed with a base oil for massage.

ROSEMARY OIL

Sweet-smelling rosemary oil is a great antiseptic to use for flu, coughs, headaches, depression, muscular stress, arthritis, rheumatism, fatigue, and forgetfulness. Rosemary oil is stimulating and will perk you up if you do a head steam with it or put a couple of drops in the bath.

HOW TO USE ESSENTIAL OILS

Most of the home remedies I prefer are either essential oil massage treatments or essential oils diffused into the bath or air.

The best base oils for essential oils are cold-pressed vegetable and seed or nut oils. The most affordable are sunflower, safflower, corn, and grapeseed. Add essential oils to base oil at a ratio of 1 drop per 5 milliliters. Twenty drops of an essential oil is approximately 1 milliliter, so add 20 drops to 100 milliliters.

A few drops of an essential oil from a dropper in the bath is sufficient for therapeutic use, and a few drops in water in a diffuser will fill a room with healing molecules. A drop on a cotton ball wiped on a lightbulb or on a radiator will also gently diffuse the oil into the air. Here's another helpful tip: try a few drops in a small bowl of very hot water. Shut the doors and windows, and the essence will permeate a room in 5 minutes. This is a particularly easy way to create a nice ambience in a room with a soothing, scented air.

My father suffers from osteoarthritis in his shoulder. He is taking baths with synergistic blends of 14 essential oils (fennel, cypress, juniper, cedarwood, sandalwood, petitgrain, pine, ginger, lavender, rosemary, black pepper, birch, nutmeg, and marjoram). These, combined with sea salt and Epsom salts, have turned him into a true believer in the amazing therapeutic effects of essential oils!

SIMPLE ESSENTIAL OIL REMEDIES

Valerie Wormwood's *The Fragrant Pharmacy* is one of my bibles for learning about essential oils. Since I've discovered essential oils and aromatherapy, I've been developing my own recipes. Often, I'll amend a recipe to just one or two oils that I have on hand.

ATHLETE'S FOOT

Use undiluted tea tree oil on the affected area or massage with 1 drop of tea tree oil in a teaspoon of vegetable oil.

CUTS

Stanch an open wound with lavender oil on a cotton ball. Bandage a cut with a drop of lavender oil on gauze, change the dressing morning and night, and leave the wound uncovered as much as possible from the third day onward.

BRUISES

Add 2 drops of lavender oil and 2 drops of rosemary oil to a bowl of hot water and the same to a bowl of cold water. Alternately apply to the bruised area a washcloth soaked in the hot infusion and one soaked in the cold infusion.

BURNS

Run the burn under cold water for 15 minutes, and then apply 2 drops of neat (undiluted) lavender oil to the burn. Cover the area with a gauze compress soaked in cold water and 3 drops of lavender oil.

BOILS

Add 3 drops of lavender oil and 3 drops of tea tree oil to a small bowl of hot water, bathing the area twice a day.

CHEST COUGH

Prepare a bowl of boiling water for inhalation with 1 drop of rosemary, 2 drops of peppermint, and 1 drop of eucalyptus. Make a massage oil for chest and back with 1 drop of lavender, 3 drops of rosemary, 4 drops of eucalyptus, and 1 drop of thyme in a level tablespoon of vegetable oil.

DRY COUGH

Make a honey and lemon hot toddy, adding 1 drop of eucalyptus. Massage chest and back with 2 drops each of eucalyptus and thyme in a level tablespoon of vegetable oil. For a head steam, add either 2 drops of lavender or 2 drops of eucalyptus to the hot water.

COLD SORES

Apply tea tree oil directly to the sore, morning and night.

COMMON COLD

Make a bowl of hot water for inhalation with 1 drop each of thyme, lavender, and eucalyptus oils. For a hot bath, add 2 drops each of thyme, lavender, and tea tree oil. Soak in the bath, relaxing your muscles and breathing deeply.

DIARRHEA

Always be sure to drink a lot of water when you are afflicted. If the cause is food related, make a drink with a teaspoon of honey in warm water and a drop of peppermint oil. If you think you have a virus or nervous tummy, make a drink with warm water, a teaspoon of honey, and a drop of eucalyptus oil.

HEADACHES

For a general headache, massage temples with a drop of either lavender or peppermint oil, or both together. You can also use rosemary or clove oil, but you will need to experiment, as some essentials will work better for you than others. If the headache is related to an upset tummy, mix a drop of peppermint oil with a teaspoon of honey dissolved in a cup of warm water, and sip slowly.

HEARTBURN

Make a drink by adding a drop of peppermint oil to a cup of warm water with a teaspoon of honey, and sip slowly. Massage the upper abdomen with 2 drops of eucalyptus and 3 drops of peppermint diluted in a teaspoon of vegetable oil.

TOOTHACHE

Place 1 drop of clove oil on a cotton swab and apply directly to the tooth and the surrounding gum. If you have a decayed tooth waiting to be treated, apply a paste made of goldenseal powder and water to the affected area. It tastes bitter but will prevent an infection from setting in until you can see a dentist.

MEDICINE CABINETRY

I've found that my remedy box has grown into a cupboard over the years. I tend to study and read up on a condition and seek out the most effective and reliably recommended remedy to treat it. Most herbs, tinctures, and essential oils have more than one therapeutic use, and my knowledge has grown as a result of having some of these herbs in my cupboard. Often, the range of uses is wide; for example, lavender oil is indicated for skin conditions, respiratory and circulation problems, nervous tension and exhaustion, coughs and colds, muscle aches, and menstrual cramps, as well as cuts. I stanched a deep cut on my toe with lavender oil recently, a new use for me, and it worked great. It's a natural disinfectant, too! I would estimate that this cure cost me about a dime as opposed to a $500 trip to a crowded emergency room, with an exposure to myriad viruses. It was peace of mind for pennies.

Because I have children, I keep a well-stocked first aid kit. Instead of expensive over-the-counter products, we use hydrogen peroxide, witch hazel, calamine lotion, aloe vera gel, and both arnica cream and calendula cream. We are (almost) ready for anything!

Creams and ointments are often expensive to buy but can be made easily at home. Here is an easy recipe to make your own curative cream.

BASIC TOPICAL OINTMENT

stainless steel saucepan, bowl, whisk, and thermometer

small clean jars or cans to store your ointment in

15 grams (1 tablespoon) beeswax

80 milliliters (5 tablespoons) organic vegetable oil (sunflower oil is effec-

tive and affordable; jojoba oil and avocado oil are nice but pricey)

tincture: add 30 drops of arnica tincture to make an arnica cream; 30 drops of calendula tincture and 10 drops of lavender oil to make calendula cream

Melt the beeswax and vegetable oil in a double boiler (or in a bowl over a saucepan). When the beeswax is fully melted, remove the bowl or pan from the heat. Whisk the ointment until it is cooled to around 100°F, then stir in the tincture you are using.

Label and store in clean lidded jars or cans. These homemade creams will last longest if you keep them refrigerated.

KITCHEN CURES

Many remedies can be made from what you have in the kitchen, from spices as well as plants. Here are a few simple tried and tested recipes:

NUTMEG

Grated nutmeg soothes diarrhea and upset tummies. Use a nutmeg grater to grate a small amount (about 1/8 teaspoon) into warmed milk (cow, soy, rice, or in oat milk).

CAYENNE

Use this pepper as a remedy for colds, coughs, sore throats, heartburn, hemorrhoids, and varicose veins, or as a digestive stimulant and to improve circulation. Make an infusion by adding ½ teaspoon cayenne powder to 1 cup boiled water. Add 2 cups of hot water to make a more pleasant and palatable infusion. Add lemon and honey to taste.

CABBAGE

This commonplace vegetable is a fantastic antibacterial and anti-inflammatory. Cabbage can be used for stomach ulcers, arthritis, and swollen joints, or as a liver tonic. To create a cabbage tonic, dilute 1 part cabbage juice with 2 parts water. For swollen joints and arthritic pain, lightly crush a few green outer cabbage leaves with a rolling pin, and then lay over afflicted area with the inner side of the leaf on your skin, securing with a bandage. Some prefer to boil the leaves, let them cool, and then apply. Going to bed with a cabbage bandage on is also good, giving the leaf time to work its magic.

BLACK AND GREEN TEAS

Use black tea for an upset tummy and diarrhea. Green tea strengthens the immune system, and you can reuse tea bags to stanch cuts or calm insect bites.

WHITE TEA

White tea, green tea, and black tea are all made from the leaves of *Camellia sinensis*. White tea is made from the youngest leaves of the plant; it is a sweet brew and has less caffeine than green or black tea. It is also rich in antioxidants and is recommended for reducing "bad" cholesterol and improving artery health. White tea is a little costly but a good choice for health and flavor.

LEMON

Use this citrus for colds and infections. Add the fresh-squeezed juice to hot water, with honey to taste. For a fast sore-throat curative, use unsweetened lemon juice with warm water as an antiseptic gargle.

TURMERIC

This spice is a natural antiseptic and antibacterial. Turmeric is also a liver detox and curative for acne and common colds. Make a turmeric tea by adding a teaspoon of the powder to 4 cups of boiling water. Simmer over low heat until it dissolves, adding milk and honey to taste.

KOMBUCHA TEA

Some people love the taste of kombucha tea; others don't relish it at all. It has been credited with miraculous properties and is a probiotic, making it very curative for digestive issues. Kombucha also comes recommended for acne, constipation, arthritis, depression, and fatigue, and is hailed as a protection against cancer. I regard it as a tasty tonic, and my family drinks it daily. My sons were the first to taste kombucha, and they loved the fizziness and flavor. This healthful drink is easy to make so long as you have a "ferment" (some people call it a "mushroom" because of the way it looks). To procure your ferment, try to find somebody who brews kombucha already. They should have plenty of ferments to share, as every batch of tea grows an extra ferment on top of the original.

- a large wide-necked glass jar, cloth or paper towel to cover jar, rubber band to secure cover
- 7 tea bags, black or green (preferably organic)
- 1 cup sugar
- 2 quarts water
- kombucha ferment

Boil the water and add it to the tea bags in the jar. Let it steep for 20 minutes.

Remove the tea bags and add the sugar, stirring to dissolve.

When the tea has cooled, add the kombucha ferment with some of the liquor that it came in, roughly 10 percent of the total tea in your jar.

Cover the jar with the cloth or paper towel, and secure with the rubber band. The lid will serve to keep dust and flies out while allowing the tea to breathe. Let the jar sit in one place (moving can disturb the fermentation process), out of the direct sunlight, and at room temperature.

The fermentation process will take seven to 12 days, depending on the room temperature. Your batch of kombucha will ferment more quickly if the room is warm. You have to check to see when it is ready, and you'll be able to tell by the taste. When fermented, the tea can be decanted into glass bottles with screw lids and kept in the fridge. Remember to keep a little of the kombucha tea to add with your ferment for your next batch.

ALL-PURPOSE AROUND-THE-HOUSE REMEDIES

STINGS

Home remedies for bee and wasp stings are just as effective as store-bought treatments. Try applying apple cider vinegar at the place of the sting to draw out the poison and stop the swelling. The common weed known as plantain (*Plantago major*) grows everywhere. The leaves, mixed with saliva or water, are laid on the sting and draw out the poison, calming the pain. Tobacco works the same way.

HEAD LICE

Home treatments for head lice are preferable to commercial treatments, as these are both toxic and expensive. Use 10 drops of tea tree, eucalyptus, or oregano oil in ½ fluid ounce of jojoba base oil. The jojoba works particularly well in loosening the eggs from the hair shaft. Apply this every night for a week or as long as needed, massaging the oil into the scalp. It isn't necessary to saturate the entire length of the hair. Check for nits and eggs in good sunlight daily, combing carefully through the hair with a metal-tooth comb. The bonus with this natural treatment for lice is that the oil will condition the hair beautifully!

SKUNK CURE

My dog Akira hasn't learned his lesson about skunks, and probably never will. Luckily, there is an easy, effective, and cheap antidote.

1 quart hydrogen peroxide 3%
¼ cup baking soda
1 tablespoon liquid soap

Combine ingredients in a plastic bucket. Using rubber gloves, scrub your sorry pet with this skunk cure, adding up to a quart of water if your dog is huge and hairy. Rinse in tepid water.

POISON OAK AND IVY CURES

While my kids occasionally need refresher courses on poison oak and ivy, the one thing they do remember is that bathing in uncooked oatmeal helps relieve the itching! This helps the sufferer and costs very little. Use oats from your kitchen, adding at least 3 cups to a bath. Baking soda in the bath will also relieve the itch and dry out oozing blisters.

CHAVANPRASH

My home remedies are drawn from a lifetime's experience and many different sources, including the lore of my English family. In my reading and study, I discovered an Ayurvedic remedy that I love, Chavanprash, a tonic made from amla leaves. Chavanprash is like a sticky black jam that you dissolve in hot water or milk. Amla (or Indian gooseberry), the main ingredient, is very high in antioxidants. Chavanprash is made from amla mixed with 49 other Ayurvedic herbs. Chavanprash is a tonic recommended for heart health, lung support, immune support, liver detox, mental clarity, constipation, and menstruation issues, and it tastes great!

I believe my family enjoys good health because we are attentive to what we eat and how we live. I estimate that we have saved thousands of dollars by using kitchen cabinet cures, teas, tonics, and tinctures. Here's to your health!

CHAPTER 3

Through the Looking Glass: Seeing Stuff Differently

FREECONOMICS

We are so used to paying for everything in Western society that the idea of a valid alternative takes a little getting used to. Take the concept of a gift economy: the famous potlatch of the Pacific Northwest native tribes is probably the best-known example. The purpose of the potlatch was redistribution and reciprocity of wealth; whoever hosted the potlatch received societal approval and ranked highly in the society. Potlatch ceremonies were banned by the US and Canadian governments in the late 19th century. As missionary William Duncan wrote in 1875, "[the potlatch is] by far the most formidable of all obstacles in the way of Indians becoming Christians or even civilized."[1]

Nevertheless, recent years have seen an uptick in the "Barter, don't buy" movement. Well-known initiatives like blood banks, where blood is donated, or Wikipedia, a collaborative online encyclopedia whose contributors are unpaid and access is free, are good examples of a gift economy in contemporary society.

In Western society we are used to thinking about economies in terms of scarcity, whereas a gift economy works on the assumption of abundance. The accessibility of the Internet has made gift economy principles easier to realize; Wikipedia, Open Source software initiatives, and many other information resources are free online.

In practice, there is only a fine line between a pure gift economy and a bartering economy. The quilting bee illustrates the point quite well. Quilters gather and volunteer to sew on one another's quilts. The implicit assumption is that eventually everybody will get help with their quilts.

The Burning Man festival (www.burningman.com) encourages gift-economy-style exchange between attendees, but entrance tickets must be purchased and a few essential commodities such as coffee and ice are paid for with currency. This gathering is the largest temporary city dedicated to art that the world has yet seen. Larry Harvey, founder of Burning Man, believes that "when you give a gift or receive a gift from someone it creates an immediate moral bond with them, this feeling of human connection. [This] is where community begins."[2]

Connecting with people and sharing resources helps individuals build community and find great enjoyment. Before considering buying anything at all, check your local resources for the free stuff!

BE A FREECYCLER

For me, the coolest of the online free resource sites is Freecycle (www.freecycle.org). The Freecycle Network initiative started in Tucson in 2003, when Deron Beal sent out the first e-mail to 30 or so friends and local nonprofits letting them know about the items he had to give away. Freecycle now has 4,738 groups worldwide and an amazing 6,690,000 members. Just think about how many wonderful free treasures have changed hands and the sheer tonnage saved from landfill. Bravo, Mr. Beal!

Freecycle's mission is to save good stuff from the landfill, promote environmental sustainability, and imbue life with the spirit of generosity, creating stronger local communities in the process.

The steps to join a Freecycle group are straightforward. If there isn't a group in your area yet, you can start one. Once you have joined your local group, you can begin to post messages for what you want and what you have to offer. Freecycle is administrated by volunteers and has the great advantage of not needing a physical location; Freecycle's easy-to-use listing website makes it nearly effortless. Some posts are for significant items such as computers, bicycles, televisions, stereos, and even cars. (Requests for SpongeBob SquarePants lunchboxes are quite common as well.) Offering your surplus and finding what you need for free are both gratifying experiences, and ultimately, they alleviate a lot of stress on our precious planet.

NAKED LADY PARTIES

You can share your surplus clothing with friends and acquaintances by throwing a "naked lady party." This is a fun way to exchange clothes as well as other items. First, set a date, and invite a group of friends to your house (we do ladies only, but men could do it too); ask everybody to bring some clothes that they don't want anymore. Set up your living room as a shop, designating different areas for guests to deposit their items—dresses in one pile, sweaters in another, and so on. Be sure to make a bedroom available for those friends who are too shy to try on clothes in company. We usually drink wine and have some snacks, and we end up with bags of new-to-us clothing. Don't be bashful—things that you are heartily sick of will be starring in somebody else's wardrobe, and the surplus will be dispatched to the thrift store, having made room for your new acquisitions.

CHANGE FOR FREE

- Start a class project for pennies: save glass jars, get some cheesecloth and rubber bands, and teach elementary-school kids how to grow sprouts.
- Why stop at naked lady parties? Organize exchange gatherings for swapping magazines, movies, baby equipment, kids' clothes, books, and toys. Pass stuff around and help keep useful items out of landfill!
- Instead of consigning your old sneakers to the trash, take them down to your local Nike store and they will recycle them into surfaces for playgrounds, athletic mats, even new sneakers. Check for details at www.nikereuseashoe.com.

THE ART OF THE SCROUNGE

Redistributing surplus has been the driving force behind many nonprofit organizations serving local communities. Research reveals who is doing what in your locale. One of my favorite initiatives is the Scroungers' Center for Reusable Art Parts, known by it's acronym, SCRAP. SCRAP has been operating in an industrial district in San Francisco since 1976. Donations of paper, paint, and all kinds of arty bits and pieces are the mainstay of SCRAP's inventory. I've seen reams of embossed ribbon, plaster casts, tubes of glitter, and circuit boards. They offer art supplies at very low cost and provide free materials for art projects through community outreach. Recently, my son found the necessary components for his animation project there: a huge piece of green fabric to make his green screen, pipe cleaners to make antennae for his animated insects, and some "eyes," all for a couple of dollars.

NEARLY FREE HOLIDAYS?

Gift economy is a really helpful concept for the budget conscious, and it can help you more than you might first imagine. It may be time to reexamine everything you thought you couldn't do and see if there is another way. Vacationing is a good example—in addition to the affordable camping/hosteling holiday options, consider couch surfing: staying at somebody's home whenever they can comfortably accommodate you. There are several online couch surfing sites where you can list your own couch and search for others in the destination of your choice. This free accommodation exchange will give you a really unique and much more personal view of a new place as well as a way to connect with people who live there. The idea is not new; Servas International (www.servas.org) was founded in 1949 and is recognized by the United Nations as a hospitality network. Check out the wildly successful and well organized CouchSurfing (www.couchsurfing.org) and Hospitality Club (www.hospitalityclub.org). And take time to look around the Web; there are many similar, smaller initiatives online catering to the budget traveler.

FREE ENTERTAINMENT

- Download free music legally. There are plenty of sites offering free music, new and old: www.kazaa.com, www.ez-tracks.com, www.betterpropaganda.com, www.degreedirectory.org.
- Download or stream movies free and legal: www.YouTube.com. www.hulu.com, www.mytheater.org.
- Many websites offer free games for kids and adults: www.pogo.com, www.freeonlinegames.com, www.net-games.biz, www.games.com.
- Read for free online; new literature and the classics are freely available online: wwwauthorama.com, www.questia.com, readprint.com, www.gutenberg.org, www.manybooks.net.
- Free children's books online: www.magickeys.com, www.bygosh.com.
- Also rediscover your local library. Even if your branch is small they will order books for you.

FREE BOXES AND MARKETS

ANONYMOUS GIFTING

A real-time venue has its own charm. Case in point: the Bolinas Free Box. This institution began 30 years ago by accident. As the story goes, a young couple were departing the shores of Bolinas, California, and dumped some boxes of extra belongings behind the community center as they left. The rather nice assortment of clothes, books, and household utensils drew some interested residents to have a look. By the end of the day, several other people had bought free stuff down to share. The Free Box took up residence in a shed between the health food store and the community center and has been providing all comers with all kinds of free fare ever since. The era of the free box was born.

FREE BOXES

The free box is a very workable concept, as the longevity of the Bolinas Free Box attests, but there are problems to be avoided. Dropping off damaged, soiled, or unusable items is inappropriate. Also, tidiness must be taken into consideration. The best-case scenario is an organized walk-in so that people can see what freebies are available. A free box initiative really needs a shed or other weatherproof shelter that people can easily access, and committed volunteers are essential to keep the stock in reasonable order.

FREE MARKETS

Akin to the fabulous free box concept is the free market. It is one of my absolute favorite examples of a gift economy, where people come together with items to give away or share. A free market can move around freely and is a lot easier to realize than a free box. The Really Really Free Market (www.reallyreally

free.org) is a great prototype. It is a pure gift economy where no money changes hands. Participants simply bring their offerings and display them communally. People also bring their expertise and talents to share: lawyers, musicians, jugglers, gardeners, ecologists, hairdressers, tarot readers, and cookie bakers are all there enjoying this unique marketplace. The free market constitutes an entirely different economic system that can provide as much diversity as the market economy, and for free!

The Really Really Free Market website lists 34 regular free markets happening in states across the US and another 10 or so worldwide in places like Perth, Australia. Yours could be the next!

FREEGANS AND STREET SHOPPING

There is plenty of free stuff, even food, to be found on the street. Urban foraging, or dumpster diving, has become very popular in the last few decades. Well-known proponents of the movement like the nonprofit organization Food Not Bombs began feeding the hungry with salvaged food 30 years ago.

The Diggers, who came together in the 1960s in San Francisco, regularly fed around 200 people a day on donated and foraged food. They also ran free shops, threw free parties, and started a free medical clinic.

Some contemporary urban foragers call themselves Freegans (a composite of "free" and "vegan") and pride themselves on their recycling prowess. The Freegans' mission is to live with minimal consumption of resources and limited involvement in the mechanisms of the conventional economy. If you fancy learning the skills necessary for successful dumpster diving, Freegans (www.freegans.info) are the people to contact. Active groups are listed, and some organize trash tours where they instruct newcomers on how to scavenge safely. The basic rules are commonsense: forage with at least one other person, always thoroughly check food when you get home and wash as needed before eating anything, and don't leave a big mess at the scene of the foraging—the rodents will love you, but store owners won't!

Street shopping is not limited to food retrieval; many perfectly usable items are thrown out daily. Serious Freegans salvage items and then redistribute what they don't need. Sometimes people put unwanted furniture outside their houses with a sign that says "Free." Keep your eyes peeled, because great stuff is there for the taking.

Check locally for free farm stands. In my neighborhood we have a local group who run a farm stand every weekend where homegrown produce is given away (www.freefarmstand.org). These urban revivalists garden in reclaimed urban lots and shared gardens; they also harvest gardens for people who don't have the time to do it themselves. At the farm stand, starter plants and seedlings are distributed, as is free advice and gardening know-how.

What might seem wild and radical is actually quite basic in human nature—the more human face of the marketplace. Free initiatives such as these are on the increase and are fun and fulfilling to get involved with. When you partake in the gift economy and live the ideal of "paying it forward," you'll love it!

FREE SCHOOLING

- Check online for instructions and procedures for all kinds of tasks. You'll find video demonstrations for anything from bookbinding (www.milliande.com, www.edenworkshops.com) to learning a foreign language (www.livemocha.com, www.babelnation.com).
- Comprehensive know-how resources online include: www.ehow.com, www.wikihow.com, www.instructables.com, www.howstuffworks.com.

REIMAGINING: START WITH WHAT YOU'VE GOT

I am utterly inspired by the spectacular grassroots Makers Movement, started by enthusiasts who combine their technological expertise with their love of arts and crafts. The Makers Faire, an event sponsored by the publishers of *Make* and *Craft* magazines, showcases the many inventive and unlikely creations that keen makers manufacture. The informal Makers Movement spokesman is Mr. Jalopy, who has created some amazing things, such as the world's biggest iPod, which is actually an old stereo that converts vinyl recordings to MP3s. Mr. Jalopy doesn't like to throw stuff away; he'd rather fix it, but usually he modifies as well as repairs. All kinds of creative collective groups show off their expertise at the Faire. The Swap-o-rama-rama takes the naked lady party idea to the next level: participants get to remake items on the spot and learn how to knit, crochet, repair, and fringe—you name it. They even provide labels for your reimagined garment that read "Modified by Me."

Before you throw out or donate stuff you are bored with, try reimagining it. I keep a box of clothes for revamping, which for me mostly turns out to mean dyeing and patching. When white or pale-color T-shirts acquire stains, I wait till I have a few and then dye them. I also dye bedraggled dishtowels, bath towels, underwear, curtains, and tablecloths—anything that needs a lift.

Beyond straight dyeing, a few simple techniques will revive even the most tired items. Silk-screening, stenciling, tie-dye, and batik can all be done cheaply at home. The older the fabric you are reimagining, the more receptive it will be to dyeing and printing. Of course, every T-shirt has its day, and there does come a point when they need to be cut up into rags. Nevertheless, it is often possible to extend the life of nicely worn-in but not altogether worn-out garments using these techniques. Black cotton clothes that have lost their blackness with frequent washing can be redyed easily and emerge looking brand new. It's amazing how the saddest garments and fabrics can get a new lease on life.

Recently, I was given a really nice single comforter cover. I thought it would be perfect for my older son, but unfortunately he wasn't crazy about the pale blue color and the woven flower pattern. I asked him if he would like it better if it was dark blue and the pattern was less obvious. This was much more appealing, so I dyed it and printed a simple "Transformers" motif on it, and now it's his favorite! I have friends who collect old T-shirts and screen-print them, and other friends who recycle clothing and revamp it with tie-dye and batik. It really isn't expensive to dye, and there are natural, nontoxic dyes and fixing agents on the market. I have rescued many a tired garment or linen by simply reinventing it in this way.

DON'T DESPAIR—REPAIR!

I'm not any kind of seamstress, but basic alterations I can do. I can take up hems, sew on buttons and patches, and I've become expert at choosing the right spot to make a perfect-length pair of cutoffs! Patching my kids' jeans has become a way of life—I keep old pairs to use for future patches. I have a patchwork quilt that I've been working on for several years. Many of the patches are from my old summer dresses and clothes the boys grew out of. It's still unfinished, but one day I will complete my "memory quilt" composed of these favorite fabrics.

Reimagining doesn't stop with clothes; unappealing old furniture in need of a face-lift can be worked with cheaply. Simply sanding down painted wood can often yield aesthetically pleasing results by exposing the actual surface of the wood. Repainting is always an option, as is staining. I particularly like stencil designs on furniture along with decoupage motifs. A furniture revamping project may turn out to be a huge investment in time, but the results will be unique and very nearly free. Decoupage is admittedly a long process of multiple steps: adhering the chosen image to the surface, varnishing, drying, sanding, and finishing. This process is repeated until the surface is smoothed. When our friend Silas's mother decoupaged a chest of drawers with Thomas the Tank Engine scraps, all the little boys drooled over it. These reimagining craft techniques may be new territory for you, but they are pretty easy. Stencils are super easy and can be cut out from thick cardstock using only an exacto blade. Decoupage starts with selecting favorite postcards, magazine images, old photographs, and so on, or as Silas's mom did, you can clean out the toy box and get creative!

THE CRAFT OF REIMAGINING

Reimagining is great for your everyday life but can also become a good source of gifts. Old trays, little boxes, chests, and lamps found at yard sales, thrift stores, or in Grandma's attic can be stenciled, painted, or decoupaged and make the most original gifts, as do screen-printed art and clothing. A few of my friends have even ended up making a business out of their expertise in these homely crafts.

ART IS FREE!

Art can inspire and inform your life. A well-placed art piece on the wall can transform a room into someplace really special. If you don't have much of a budget for buying art, think about making some. Folks with young kids are mostly happy to have their children's masterpieces up. Framing favorite drawings will extend the life of these works of art and make the kids (and parents) very proud.

Photographs you love can be blown up and framed, bringing your unique sense of beauty and meaning to your home or workplace. You can get really creative with this idea, too. I know a married couple who work on art pieces together. He paints images and she adds the words. They work on large canvases and also experiment with glass and other mediums. Their artwork is beautiful and inspiring. While homemade artworks are not necessarily going to accrue value in the art market, it doesn't mean they aren't amazing, special, and precious to us, and that is equally valuable.

Since the advent of conceptual art, what constitutes a work of art is utterly open: urinals, bricks, found objects, stuffed toys, flashing lightbulbs on a time switch—really, anything goes! I particularly like collages, but I envy those with the eye to find a sculpture in a great piece of driftwood or a twisted tree root, or the patience to collect sea glass for a mosaic.

Appropriation is a valid artmaking technique these days. If you fancy a Warhol, screen-print your own version. Spin paintings, once the exclusive domain of elementary-school kids, have been appropriated by Damien Hirst—are you next? Make a butterfly painting with a few preserved butterflies discovered at the neighborhood yard sale. Place them on a wet canvas painted with regular household paint and they'll stick. Voilà!—your own beautiful, affordable art. Ideas are free; use them guiltlessly for your own pleasure and enjoy making your own art.

People are always commenting on the art we have in our house: paintings, collages, and a lot of clay pieces done when the boys were younger. As playwright Jean Anouilh once wrote, "Things are beautiful when you love them." I think that anything you love to look at should be out on display. I have a beautiful Afghan dress that my godmother gave me for my 16th birthday; it's patchwork and quite flamboyant, and I rarely get an opportunity to wear it, so instead I hang it on my bedroom wall suspended from a length of gardening bamboo through the sleeves. Now I get to admire it every day!

Here are some of my tried and true techniques for reimagining—taking an object and reinventing it for a whole new incarnation and use. I have saved thousands of dollars over the years and greatly enjoyed the creativity in learning new crafts.

BASIC DYEING TIPS

PREDYEING

I recommend a predyeing soak in soda ash, also known as washing soda or sodium carbonate (you can get it at a hardware store).

soda ash

fiber-reactive dye

5-gallon plastic container to dye in

Add 1 cup of soda ash to 1 gallon of water and let the fabric steep for 20 minutes or so. This makes the fibers more absorbent for the dye, recommended if your fabric is not 100 percent cotton or is not a natural fiber. If there is any synthetic content, the soda ash soak will help your colors take.

Silk also benefits from the soda ash presoak, but after rinsing, let the silk steep in 1 gallon of water with 1 cup of distilled vinegar to restore acidity.

HOW TO MAKE A SCREEN PRINT

You'll need to procure a few supplies to make your own screen print. You can get everything from the art supply store, or you can improvise.

Buy old picture frames with a flat front side; carefully take the glass out and set aside. To cover the screen, you'll need to buy mesh screen fabric from an art supply store. There are different mesh counts for paper and fabric printing, or you can use a piece of gauzy curtain fabric with a close weave.

screen frame (art supply store) or old picture frame
mesh screen (art supply store) or thin gauze fabric with tight weave
office stapler and staples
photo emulsion and activator (art supply store)
cardboard for making a squeegee (art supply store)
a piece of glass to cover the screen
black fabric
screen-printing ink (art supply store)

Cut the mesh or fabric an inch or two bigger than your frame, and then cover the front side of the frame. It's helpful to have an extra pair of hands to help get a tight stretch: staple one side, making sure the fabric is as straight to the frame as possible, and then stretch it to the opposite side and staple. Cut off the excess fabric, but not too close to the staples, so the fabric doesn't fray and the screen doesn't come loose.

Follow the instructions on the box to mix the photo emulsion with the activator in the right proportion. Spread photo emulsion on the screen. Cut some cardboard scrapers using the sides from cereal boxes, and spread the emulsion evenly on both sides of the screen. Do not spread the emulsion thickly; remove any excess with your cardboard scraper and return it to the emulsion bottle.

The screen now needs to dry in a dark location; a closet, basement, or garage will work nicely.

As soon as the emulsion is dry, you should burn your image onto the screen—otherwise the emulsion will harden and won't wash off. Take the screen outside in daylight and lay it front side down on some black fabric. Place your transparency or stencil onto the screen and hold it flat with a piece of glass smaller than the frame. When the emulsion changes color from light green to blue, it has hardened. Everywhere the sun doesn't reach the screen the emulsion will wash out, so your stencil or transparency needs to be opaque.

When the newly blue emulsion has hardened, wash it off with running water, ideally a pressurized garden hose.

When you have washed the screen, take it back into the sun and let the remaining emulsion dry and harden up. This extra step will make the screen stronger.

Homemade screens tend to be weakest at the edges, so make a border with masking tape on the front side to prevent the ink leaking through.

You will need a stable flat surface to print on. Lay down layers of newspaper to protect the surface, and then the paper or fabric to be printed. If you are screening a garment, put paper inside it so the ink doesn't seep through to the back. Place the screen over your paper or fabric and pour a little printing ink in a line at the top of the screen. Using a squeegee or a clean piece of straight-edged cardboard, draw the ink down firmly and evenly over the screen, going right to the bottom of the screen. Scoop any excess ink off the screen at the bottom with a piece of cardboard and return as much as you can to the bottle.

Lift the screen and dry your print. If you have printed on fabric, cover it with paper and iron over the print when dry to fix the image.

You will be amazed at how effective screen-printing is. The last batch of screen-print T-shirts we made at our Peace Club are highly sought-after pieces!

SIMPLE TIE-DYE

Tie-dye is a great way to save stained clothing and makes a fun project for kids.

soda ash
fiber-reactive dye
rubber bands
squirt bottles
clothing to dye

Take a clean, dry garment and tie it off. Using rubber bands, you can tie off the fabric any way you like: for a circular design, pull up fabric and make a pointed tent shape, tie off the bottom tightly and then tie upward, adding ties until you run out of fabric. The best thing to do is experiment! When you've tied as much as you want, soak it for 30 minutes in a soda ash solution of 1 cup to 1 gallon of water. This is not an essential step, but it improves the fix of the dye to the fabric.

Prepare your dye and decant it carefully into squirt bottles. Protect the surface and area you are working on with newspaper, and then start applying the dye to your tied-up garment. Just squeeze dye around your ties and let the dye soak into the layers of fabric. When you have finished applying the dye put the garment in a plastic bag to prevent it from drying out, and leave it overnight.

Rinse off the excess dye and then wash the garment a couple of times in a washing machine. (Of course, nothing else should be in the same load!)

EASY DECOUPAGE

There are all kinds of products designed for decoupage, but really all you need is white glue, an exacto knife, and some images that you have selected.

white glue
exacto craft knife
paper scraps, images

Make sure that whatever surface you are going to decoupage is clean and dry. You may even want to paint the surface first depending on the effect you are going for.

Next, carefully cut out your chosen images, letting your imagination run wild. These can come from greetings cards, magazines, wallpaper, wrapping paper, or old postcards. I have decoupaged poems cut out of an old book, vintage stamps, and fortunes from fortune cookies!

With a little cardboard spreader or small paintbrush, coat the back of an image with glue, put a little glue on the surface where you will position the image, and stick the image in place. With your spreader or brush, apply glue to the top surface of the image. When the glue has dried, check to see if the edges have firmly adhered. If not, add another layer of glue until the edges of the image are flush to the surface. Repeat with the remaining images.

It you are working with a large object such as a chest of drawers, you'll need to switch to clear varnish instead of white glue. Also, be patient with the process. The varnish takes a good few hours to dry, and subsequent layers of varnish need to be applied until you have the desired effect. For a smoother, glossier surface, you can sand down the varnish between layers; this is optional. I strongly suggest you use one of the nontoxic clear varnishes on the market. Nevertheless, it's a good precaution to work in the open air or in a well ventilated area.

A few years ago, I acquired some vintage box files. They were sturdy and in good condition, so I customized them with decoupaged images chosen with the recipients in mind. Personalizing gifts like this is very much appreciated; my friend Barbara loves her "letter box" with its photos of her son and cutout motifs from a piece of Escher wrapping paper. I love rescuing images from magazines in the recycling and making arty gifts with them.

EASY BATIK

beeswax
paraffin (optional)
double boiler (or an electric skillet or old fondue pot)
paintbrush
fiber-reactive dye
cookie sheet

Lay your fabric or garment on a flat surface. If you are working on a piece of clothing, place a cookie sheet or other "wax catcher" under it so the wax can drip through. Use a crayon or pencil to lightly mark your design on the fabric.

Prepare the wax. Because of my environmental orientation, I don't use paraffin in my wax, even though paraffin enhances the crinkly effect of batik. I think it looks fine without it! If you want to use paraffin, add 1 part paraffin to 2 parts beeswax. Gently melt the wax over low heat in an old fondue pot, double boiler, or electric skillet.

When the wax is melted to transparency, start brushing it onto the fabric. Keep dipping the brush in the wax so it doesn't harden on the brush. Make sure the wax goes through to the other side of the fabric. Be prepared for a few random drips—all wax on the fabric will become part of the final design! When your design is complete and set on, put the garment aside and let the wax dry completely.

Prepare the fiber-reactive dye according to the instructions. When the dye bath is ready, scrunch the fabric into a ball—it is this step that produces the crinkle effect. If you are not using paraffin in the wax, scrunch it up even more to get good crinkles.

Allow the piece to steep in the dye bath for at least 20 minutes, and then rinse with cold water. Hang your piece outside on a clothesline to drip-dry; don't wring it out.

When the fabric is dry, you need to remove the wax. One excellent method is covering the fabric with a sheet of newspaper and running a hot iron over it. The method that works best for me is simmering the fabric in a large cooking pot filled with water and liquid soap. It's easy—the wax lifts off and hardens on the surface, where it can be scooped off. Mind you, this method will not ruin a cooking pot, even if you use the paraffin mix. Just wash it well after use.

I have a batik session once a year or so, and I've gained some favorite garments and curtains using this easy craft.

STENCILING

Stenciling is a really easy decorative technique that looks great on walls, furniture, and fabric; most surfaces are receptive to stencils. Most people cut their stencils from some kind of acetate, but Mylar is the stencil material commonly sold in craft stores. Copy centers can make laminates of artwork, and this plastic is particularly nice and light for stencil use. I use stiff cardstock from old files, and it has worked very well for me. Acrylics are the most commonly used paints for stenciling, and they'll work on most surfaces, but glass, metal, and vinyl work better with enamel paints.

acetate and Mylar or parchment-type cardboard for making stencil
exacto craft knife
masking tape
acrylic paint
paintbrush and/or sponge

Cut your stencil using an exacto craft knife to make sure the edges you cut are clean. Remember to be really careful working with sharp blades, especially when the cardstock or acetate is tough to work with.

Place the stencil over the desired surface and tape it with masking tape so it doesn't move while you are applying the paint. The paint can be applied with a paintbrush, cotton balls, a sponge, or anything else you fancy trying. The important thing is not to overpaint, because the excess will invariably bleed under the stencil; the brush or sponge should feel dry, not dripping.

Experiment with your paint application before you do the real thing: some people like a stippling effect, where the paint is dabbed on evenly, others prefer a light swirling application. Acrylic paints work well with fabrics (particularly upholstery fabrics) and many a disfiguring stain can be obscured this way!

ALTERNATIVE AESTHETICS

I don't have a dinner service with six matching place settings, but I do have enough cups, plates, and bowls for a dinner party. When we serve dinner, our table is set with uniquely pretty plates. Friends have favorite plates and bowls at our house, and it's common knowledge that the fork with the faux-Aztec design is Daddy's.

Our mix-and-match aesthetic comes from not wanting to spend a lot of money unnecessarily. Plus, there are plenty of serviceable items available for free or nearly free! Most of our furniture and appliances are secondhand, either bought or acquired free, and they all function effectively.

Sometimes we do buy new things, but usually when we've exhausted our options. Being mindful of our impact on the environment by reusing is a powerful factor. We need to remember not to be wasteful and to conserve our natural resources whenever we can.

Our dinner plates are a good illustration of my position: our tableware is a creative collection of hand-me-downs, yard sale treasures, and gifts. We all love the eclectic effect. Our home is cozy, warm, and attractive. It is a "hands-on" house that doesn't look like anybody else's. Our home reflects us, as any home should.

NOTES

1. Robin Fisher, *Contact and Conflict: European Relations in British Columbia 1774–1890*, University of British Columbia Press (1977), 207.
2. Larry Harvey, "La Vie Bohème: A History of Burning Man," lecture given at the Walker Art Center, Minneapolis, February 24, 2000.

CHAPTER 4

Homely Habitats

However humble your home might be, you can easily create an attractive and comfortable environment in which to live. If you own your home, you can be more expansive with your plans than if you rent. Even without major eco-renovation you can make your home more energy-efficient and less toxic with relatively low expenditure.

It is unacceptable to me that our culture has arrived at a point where our homes are often created with and maintained by toxic products. The good news is that information has become increasingly available about household contamination, and while legislation is still lagging, we can take the initiative in detoxifying our homes ourselves.

For me, becoming a mother set me on a revolutionary path. When I had my first son, we lived in a warehouse loft in San Francisco's Mission District. I began to wonder about the suitability of the warehouse as a home for our baby. We had moved in during my pregnancy, and I hadn't thought much about the building's proximity to busy city streets and a six-lane freeway. Rather, my attention was focused on the cityscape views and the 5-minute walk to the Museum of Modern

Art. Down at the health clinic, seeing our street address prompted our practitioner to suggest that our son be tested for lead levels. I felt lucky when the test showed normal lead levels in our toddler, but the experience opened my eyes to the potential for pollution. I began to look at my home differently.

I approached my newfound eco-consciousness with the preconceived notion that maintaining a green home would entail spending a lot of money buying environmentally friendly products. In my search, I found that eco-products are often underrepresented in the supermarket chains, where eco-friendly options are not competitively priced beside the conventional products. However, the open secret about your basic, essential eco–home cleaning kit is that everything in it is cheap and available everywhere! Here are all the tricks of the trade I learned as an "ecomom" and founder of an eco-cleaning business.

ECO-CLEANING BASICS

The healthiest and cheapest way to clean your home is to use natural products. Nothing in your cleaning kit has to have a cautionary warning on it!

If you haven't already abandoned conventional cleaning products, do so now: they are expensive and toxic! The AAPCC (American Association of Poison Control Centers) reports that the highest number of poisonings came from conventional cleaning products in 1993 (AAPCC 1993 Report). Many side effects—headaches, allergies, even dizziness and nausea—have been noted from the use of chemical cleaning products in the home. The EPA (US Environmental Protection Agency) states that the average American home has 2–5 times more air pollution inside than the air immediately outside the house.

Eliminate this kind of pollution from your home now!

YOUR BASIC CLEANING KIT

distilled vinegar (apple cider vinegar is OK but distilled is cheaper)

baking soda

coarse salt (some people prefer salt for cutting grease and scrubbing)

borax

Bon Ami (this is my favorite brand)

Castile soap

essential oils

hydrogen peroxide 3%

cream of tartar

2 long-handled vegetable/dish scrubbing brushes (one for the toilet, one for everywhere else)

old toothbrushes

rags from old towels, T-shirts, or any nonsynthetic clothes

newspaper (crinkle it up for buffing windows and mirrors)

microfiber cloth or duster

spray bottles

rubber gloves

ECO-CLEANING TIPS AND RECIPES

The following recipes are very adaptable. I've cleaned my whole house with just a spray bottle of vinegar and a little liquid soap, so don't worry if you don't have all the ingredients.

Stick with these natural cleaning agents: baking soda, borax, Bon Ami, and coarse salt. They can all substitute for each other, and they are perfect for scouring.

Borax (sodium borate) is a mineral and a salt of boric acid. It is toxic in large doses, as is baking soda or salt, but it makes a great cleanser for around the house and in the laundry. Borax is also an effective deodorizer for furniture, carpets, and clothes, and it works as an antimold agent. I even use it as an ant deterrent! If you have really crusty pots and pans, borax is a terrific nonscratching scourer. Lift heavy fabric stains and odors by soaking the cloth in borax and water. If you are dealing with upholstery, cover the stained area with a thick paste of borax and water; use ⅓ cup borax to ½ cup water, allow to dry, and then vacuum off.

Baking soda (bicarbonate of soda) works well for all the same applications as borax, also for removing silver tarnish. Place a piece of aluminum foil in a glass bowl with 2 tablespoons of baking soda and boiling water. The tarnished items must be touching the aluminum foil; a chemical reaction causes the sulfur atoms on the tarnished silver to migrate to the aluminum foil. Baking soda and water also make a very effective vegetable wash—just sprinkle soda into a bowl of water and let your vegetables soak for a few minutes, then rinse.

Bon Ami is a natural nonscratch scourer made with calcite, feldspar, a biodegradable detergent, and a little baking soda. It's cheap and works well for scouring.

Some people swear by scouring with salt, but I only scrub with it if there's nothing else around. I do like how it absorbs oil and grease. It is also great for stove-top goop.

If I could only use one item to clean with, it would be vinegar. It deals with stains, grease, and mold, and it's a natural disinfectant. Lavender oil is my go-to essential oil because it smells so good and is also a natural disinfectant. When I make up a surface cleaner with borax or baking soda and soap, I always add drops of lavender oil.

Make up your cleaners in small batches. I suggest one spray bottle at a time; no preservatives means the shelf life of homemade cleaners is short. And always shake well before using.

ECO-PET TIPS

- Make your own cat litter using strips of newspaper or shredded paper.
- Keep chickens if you can. They are fun to take care of, especially for kids, and their free-range eggs are the best!
- Use fresh aloe on your pet's cuts.
- To treat an infected wound, use witch hazel, or dilute 5 drops of Echinacea and goldenseal tincture with 1 cup of water.
- To deter fleas, dab a little eucalyptus oil on your dog's collar.
- Or make an herbal flea collar with essential oils. Soak a natural fiber rope in 2 tablespoons of any of the following: peppermint oil, rosemary oil, citronella oil, or eucalyptus oil. Soak the rope for an hour, air-dry it, and then tie it around your dog's neck.
- Another option for deterring fleas is to make a rosemary infusion. Pour a quart of boiling water over a cup of fresh rosemary and steep for an hour. Strain it and saturate your dog's coat with the liquid. Let it air-dry. Repeat every few days in flea season.
- Use tincture of slippery elm or slippery elm tea to treat a dog with a sensitive stomach. Use 5 drops of tincture in 2 cups of warm water, or make a little slippery elm tea (½ teaspoon to 1 cup water) and pour a cup of it over food when cool.

KITCHEN CLEANING RECIPES

I think that it's especially important not to use anything toxic in the kitchen, where we prepare our food. Just remember that vinegar is a natural disinfectant. So keeping a spray bottle of it around is a great way to keep everything really clean. Spray your chopping boards daily with vinegar.

GENERAL-PURPOSE SURFACE ECO-CLEANER

This can be used on all surfaces in the kitchen, bathroom, and beyond.

1 teaspoon liquid Castile soap
1 teaspoon borax or baking soda
3 drops essential oil or a squeeze of fresh lemon juice
1 quart warm water

Mix ingredients, pour into a spray bottle, and shake well. Add 1 cup of vinegar if there is a lot of grease to deal with, and remember to use warm water.

WINDOW AND MIRROR CLEANER

Mix 1 part vinegar, 1 part water in a spray bottle. For extra "eco-action," use folded old newspaper for drying and shining.

COPPER POLISHING

You can clean copper pans by sprinkling plain salt on the surface and rubbing it with half a lemon. I used to clean a client's copper sink by coating it with a big container of plain natural yogurt. I'd let it sit for about half an hour, until the yogurt turned green. Then I'd wipe the yogurt away, and the copper would shine brilliantly.

DRAIN CLEANER

½ cup baking soda or borax
1 cup vinegar

Mix together, pour into the drain, and cover. Let it sit and fizz for 20 minutes.

Pour in ½ gallon boiling water.

If this fails to open the drain, do it again and let it sit for longer.

OVEN CLEANER

Cleaning an oven without chemicals is not difficult, but it takes time. The best way is to leave the natural cleanser on overnight.

2 cups baking soda or borax
spray bottle filled with water
spray bottle filled with white vinegar
1 tablespoon liquid Castile soap
an old sponge and a long-handled scrub brush

Spray the interior of the oven with water, then sprinkle baking soda over the bottom liberally so its completely covered. Mix 1 part baking soda and 1 part vinegar to make a paste, and coat the interior surfaces of the oven with it. Leave it on overnight.

Spray again with water in the morning. If the oven is coated with cooking oil, spray with both water and vinegar. Wipe off with soapy sponges and a long-handled scrub brush. Keep spraying water and using clean cloths to remove the buildup. Make sure to rinse with clean water at the end to leave no soap or soda behind.

If you're in a hurry, or just notice a couple of unclean spots in the oven, spray with vinegar and water, cover with baking soda, and let sit for a few minutes. Then spray on more vinegar and water and clean away the dirt with a soapy sponge.

FLOOR CLEANER

This recipe works well on vinyl, linoleum, tile, or stone floors.

1 cup vinegar
a few drops essential oil
1 gallon warm water

Apply with a mop or washrag, and rinse off with clean water. If floors need extra cleaning, try adding ½ cup of borax or baking soda to the recipe.

BATHROOM ECO-CLEANING

However basic your bathroom is, it can always be perfectly pleasant if it's clean and it smells good. Lavender oil smells wonderful in the bathroom and is an excellent deodorizing disinfectant for the task of cleaning the toilet. Lemon or grapefruit oil is good for use in the bathroom as well, and the citrus scent is very refreshing.

Use the "general-purpose surface eco-cleaner" recipe on page 83 to clean porcelain, tile, linoleum, and any woodwork in the bathroom. Essential oils are simply the best.

NATURAL TOILET CLEANER

Before you clean the toilet, pour a gallon of water into the bowl to flush out the water. It is much easier to clean when empty.

½ cup baking soda or borax
10 drops lavender, grapefruit, or lemon oil

Mix together in a bowl with enough water to make a thick paste.

Brush the paste all over the bowl and rim. Spray heavily with vinegar, either neat or with equal parts water, and leave on for 10 minutes.

Scrub the surfaces, rinse, and wipe dry. Clean as a whistle!

MOTHER NATURE'S MOLD TREATMENT

Showers often suffer recurring mold, as do bathrooms with poor ventilation. Spraying straight vinegar or a 50/50 vinegar and water solution on moldy areas is 99 percent effective. I recommend a weekly preventive vinegar spraying in mold-prone rooms.

Another great natural recipe for mold calls for lavender oil, tea tree oil, or grapefruit seed extract. These lovely essential oils all have antifungal properties and are natural disinfectants. Mix 10 drops of one of these oils with 2 cups of water, and use in a spray bottle.

I add one of these essential oils to a vinegar bottle just for extra efficacy!

AROUND THE HOUSE

A good vacuum cleaner will save you a lot of time and energy when you are housecleaning. I recommend that you get a bagless model with attachments to make it easy to get under furniture, into corners, and up the walls.

Long-handled dusters are handy for getting high up, but I favor microfiber cloths for dusting surfaces and decorative objects. Microfiber cloths, which you can wash repeatedly, are not cheap but last forever and just pick up the dust without the use of any kind of product. This is super eco and super cheap!

THE GOOD WOOD FLOOR CLEANER

1 teaspoon vinegar
1 teaspoon vegetable oil
6 drops essential oil
1 quart warm water

Mix ingredients, pour into a spray bottle, and shake well. Spray the floor and mop with a clean mop. Mop again thoroughly with clean hot water.

Buff by walking on dry flannel rags infused with a few drops of citrus essential oil. Your floors will look nice and smell even better!

"ECO-DECO" FURNITURE POLISH

Lemon oil is traditionally used for furniture because it is lubricating and also antiseptic. Avoid linseed oil preparations, as they often contain synthetic drying chemicals. Use this solution for all your wood furniture and hardwood floors.

1 cup lemon juice
10 drops lemon oil
1 tablespoon olive oil or jojoba oil
1 tablespoon water

Apply gently with a soft, clean, recycled flannel rag. Let the polish sit for 5 minutes, then buff with a soft cloth. Nothing looks or smells better than wood furniture polished with lemon!

CENTS-ABLE LAUNDRY

Laundry can be a costly business both financially and environmentally. The expensive conventional detergents and laundry aids are mostly derived from petroleum and often contain chemical fragrances and phosphates, which are known to deplete water of oxygen. This has devastating effects on fish—they basically starve and die. Eco-alternatives are much cheaper, just as effective, and so much better for our world.

At the store, look for phosphate-free, eco-friendly laundry detergent powder. The green brands use a soap base instead of petroleum, which works just as well without the deadly chemicals.

ECO-LAUNDRY TIPS

- For smart stain removal, acting quickly is always the best policy. Table salt will draw out red wine and coffee. Simply grab it off your table and pour it on the spill.
- Presoak stained fabric in a cold water bath with borax, baking soda, or vinegar. When you wash, use cold water only, as heat will "set" the stain.
- I say you never need to use the hot wash cycle in your washer. Washing with cold water saves 80–90 percent of the energy used to run a washer load.
- Always wash a full load to make your laundry more cost-effective. Eco-smarts almost always save money.
- You don't need bleach to whiten fabric; use borax instead. Add up to a cup to your washer load.
- Instead of chemical-laden fabric softener, add ½ cup of baking soda to the final rinse cycle.
- For dingy white socks, try boiling them for 10 minutes in a big cooking pot with a sliced lemon; hang dry on the line, and the sun will whiten them even more!
- Air-drying laundry extends the life of your clothes and saves a lot of energy and expense. Turn colored fabrics inside out to prevent fading from sunlight.

LITTLE HELPERS

- Buy rechargeable batteries. You'll soon cover the cost of the recharger.
- Wrap your water heater in a blanket to conserve warmth.
- Have your furnace checked yearly to make sure it's running efficiently.
- In hot weather, pull your shades down to keep the house cool instead of using air-conditioning or electric fans.

ECO-DECO

Take steps to cut down your indoor air pollution by decorating with eco-friendly products. Remember that most new furniture, including couches and chairs, soft furnishings, ready-made furniture, self-assembly kits, and carpets, is treated with chemicals containing formaldehyde, a cause of respiratory problems. Wherever possible, outgas your new items by leaving them outside in the fresh air for a day or two. New fabric, even clothing, is also chemically treated. Washing garments and linens before use removes the chemicals, but soaking fabric in baking soda and cold water for a day also does a very thorough job. When new carpets are installed, treat them by sprinkling baking soda generously over the entire area and leave for at least an hour before vacuuming. I also recommend renting a carpet shampoo machine from the supermarket and cleaning new carpeting. Instead of using chemical carpet shampoo, I use hot water mixed with 30 drops of lavender oil and put this into the carpet shampooer. This will wash out chemicals and leave the carpet smelling much sweeter. Now you can breathe easier, literally.

MARY-BETH'S RAG RUG METHOD

There are various methods of making rag rugs but Mary-Beth's technique is my favorite. She uses yarn and all different types of fabric, creating rugs that fall into the works-of-art category. To make a rug from fabric rags, pick old clothes, curtains, or other fabric and cut into 2-inch-wide strips with sharp, sturdy scissors. Make the strips as long as you can—long strips are optimal because you are going to be crocheting with them. Once you get into the rhythm of cutting strips, you'll be able to go around corners and cut really long ones.

You'll need an outsize crochet hook, which is cheap to buy at craft stores. Start crocheting with a long strip, and when you run out, tie another strip on and continue to crochet. If you are using yarn, braid it together before crocheting. These rugs are durable and truly unique.

PLANET-POSITIVE PAINTING

A quick coat of paint can transform a house, especially if the walls are dingy and marked. But do make sure that you use low-VOC or preferably non-VOC paint to avoid the side effects from regular VOC paint.

VOCs, or volatile organic compounds, are solvents released into the air as the paint dries. VOCs can cause headaches and dizziness, and according to the US Environmental Protection Agency, some VOCs are suspected carcinogens.

Conventional VOC paint has up to 10,000 chemicals in it, 300 of which are known toxins and 150 of which are linked to cancer (source: Chadderdon, greenfeet.net). There is a long list of undesirable ingredients in conventional house paint, including formaldehyde, benzene, toluene, vinyl chloride, ethyl, and mercury. The chemicals that create that "new paint" smell are dibutyl and diethyl phthalate, both extremely volatile compounds. None of this belongs in your home!

When VOC paint is freshly applied to the walls of your home, the air pollution increases a thousandfold (source: Pennock, Green Home Guide). The worst part is the lengthy period for the outgassing of the VOC paint. According to the EPA's Capstone Report, standard latex paint outgases for three and a half years! The effects can be very harmful and should be avoided at all costs.

Thus, try washing dull and dirty walls. Use a mix of liquid soap and either borax or baking soda in warm water. Use a sponge for the actual cleaning, and never use a brush or hard scrubber, as this will literally scrape the paint off the walls.

For interior painting use low-VOC or non-VOC paint. Thankfully, nowadays this is much more available from mainstream paint suppliers and is becoming more competitively priced. There are also natural paints on the market: milk paint, soy paint, and other additive-free choices. These may cost more but are worth checking into for the health and environmental benefits alone.

Homemade interior paint is cheap and easy to make and is truly additive-free.

HOMEMADE ECO-PAINT

2 cups wheat flour (any flour will work; some prefer results with bleached flour)
6–7 cups cold water
3 cups boiling water
1 cup screened clay (art supply store)
½ cup mica filler (art supply store)
natural dye (optional)

Mix the flour with 4 cups of cold water in a large mixing bowl, preferably with a whisk.

Add the flour mixture to a pot containing 3 cups of boiling water, and cook over low heat for 10 minutes. Remove from heat and add 2–3 cups of cold water.

Mix the clay and filler together dry and whisk into the flour mixture. Natural dyes such as cochineal or turmeric, tea, or berry or plant stains can be added at this point for the coloration of your choice.

Grab a brush and go for it!

SIMPLE NATURAL DYE

With a mortar and pestle, gently crush the material of your choice—berries, flowers, or leaves.

Cover with ¼ inch of water in a small saucepan and simmer until your desired shade is visible. Make sure to keep the material covered with around ¼ inch of water at all times. Try not to bring it to a boil; a slow simmer produces the deepest and most vivid shades.

Cool and strain through a cheesecloth. Discard or compost the solid material and pour the dye into an airtight container. This will keep for months if properly sealed, or better yet, use your homemade dye in a creative project immediately.

Homemade paint will often have a textured appearance depending on the type of filler that you choose. It will also be too thick to apply with a roller, so just use regular paintbrushes, preferably with natural bristles. If you want a uniform surface, you can wipe away brush streaks with a damp sponge once it starts to dry. You can also sand off paint streaks with fine-grade sandpaper when dry. Try experimenting with this rich, textural painting effect—it has the potential to look lovely and quite distinctive.

ECO-PAINT STRIPPER

If you are stripping furniture, do it outside and rinse afterward with a pressurized hose. Never use this mixture on oak wood; it will blacken on contact with washing soda. Wear rubber gloves—the washing soda may irritate your skin.

7 ounces washing soda (see Basic Dyeing Tips, page 66)
⅔ cup flour
1 quart warm water

Dissolve the washing soda in 2 cups of cold water. In a separate container, mix the flour with the warm water until it has a gel-like consistency. Combine the two mixtures.

With a sponge, apply to the surface to be stripped, using a paintbrush for tricky molding. Leave the stripper on for 30 minutes.

Rinse with water and scrub vigorously.

THERMAL HEAT METHOD

Electric thermal heat guns also do a great job of stripping away paint. The heat gun softens the paint, making it easy to scrape off with a putty knife. Be careful not to overheat and scorch the paint, as this will not be easy to remove!

BRUSH CLEANER

Boil 3 cups of vinegar. Place your paintbrushes in the hot vinegar and let them simmer for 10 minutes. Wash them in warm soapy water, rinse in cold water, and air-dry. They are ready for use!

If you rent your home and painters are coming, be sure to let your property manager or landlord know that they need to use non-VOC paint. Non-VOC paint doesn't smell, which makes for a healthy and pleasant environment as soon as it dries. Cleanup is simplified because non-VOC paints are not hazardous materials. You do not want to expose your family and friends to those harmful chemicals!

VOC contamination is endemic in conventional household building and decorating materials. It is possible to find eco–paint thinners and strippers and even eco-varnish for floors. While these are not necessarily the cheapest products, they will greatly improve the air quality and general healthiness of your home.

AIR-PURIFYING PLANTS

An excellent way to deal with indoor air pollution is to live with some air-purifying plants. NASA's Clean Air Study researched houseplants that improve air quality by humidifying and removing toxins. The areca palm gets the top score as the most effective air humidifier, while the rubber plant is best at removing chemical toxins, especially formaldehyde. Choose from any or all of these high-scoring air-purifying houseplants to improve your indoor air quality: lady palm, bamboo palm, dracaena, English ivy, dwarf date palm, ficus "Alii," Boston fern, and peace lily. Beauty with the bonus of cleaner air!

ENERGY-SAVING TIPS

If you own your home, many useful eco-renovations will save you expense and improve the quality of your home environment. They will probably increase the resale value of your home as well. Solar panels, low-flush toilets, and nontoxic materials and paints for interior decoration are a few of the easiest ways to save. Renters can also do plenty of things to be more energy efficient and save a lot of money.

Simply unplugging electrical appliances can make a significant difference to your electricity bill, because plugged-in appliances draw "standby power." The consumption of standby power by these "energy vampires" accounts for 10 percent of residential electricity nationally. To make unplugging easier, use a power strip or surge protector so you can switch everything off together. This also saves wear and tear on your outlets.

Heat loss contributes to high energy bills, so do what you can to insulate. Caulking drafty gaps around doors and windows is a good place to start. Identify the precise location of a draft by holding a lighted incense stick to window and door frames to see where the incense smoke is blown. Use a nontoxic, 100 percent silicon caulk in a caulking gun and fill up those gaps!

Big windows are great for letting in natural light, but single-pane windows lose a lot of heat. Blackout curtains help conserve heat or keep things cool depending on the season. They are inexpensive to buy, or you can make your own using a dark fabric glued or sewn to a close-weave canvas lining. Blackout curtains also cut down noise pollution substantially and keep a bedroom nice and dark even when it's sunny outside.

Appliances use a lot of electricity, but new energy-saving models are making significant reductions in bills. Call your utility company to come and test your appliances for efficiency, so you can take action accordingly.

Laptop computers use 75 percent less power than desktop models—a significant saving. Likewise, a digital radio uses significantly less power than your traditional radio. Study up and save money.

DOOR SAUSAGES

Also known as "draft stoppers," door sausages are easy to make and effectively block a draft coming in under the door. Sew a tube the width of the drafty door or window using a thick fabric; I find that the leg of an old pair of jeans can work well. Stitch up one end of your tube and fill it with cat litter, sand, old socks, scraps of fabric, or rolled sheets of newspaper.

We had door sausages made of old velvet curtains when I was a child; they were cozy!

PULL THE PLUG!

- Most appliances use energy even when they are not in use. Keep them unplugged, or use a power strip to easily turn many appliances on simultaneously.
- Make a habit of switching off lights when rooms are empty. If you have a need for an all-night light somewhere around the house, change the bulb to low-wattage and save that way.
- If you have a yard or space for a clothesline or clothes horse outside, utilize sun and wind by air-drying your laundry. You will save energy and save your clothes, as dryers are notorious for tiring out fabric.

ECO-LIGHTING

Switching from regular incandescent lightbulbs to compact fluorescent bulbs (CFLs) will save you money. The US Department of Energy recommends CFL bulbs over incandescents, and estimates that a CFL will save you about $30 over its lifetime and pay for itself in about six months. DOE states that a CFL uses 75 percent less energy and lasts about 10 times longer than an incandescent bulb (www.energystar.gov/index.cfm?c=cfls.pr_cfls).

Unlike conventional bulbs, CFLs do contain a very small amount of mercury, a toxic pollutant. The EPA estimates that there is 4–5 milligrams of mercury in an average CFL household bulb, an amount that can be cleaned up safely if a bulb breaks in your house.

BROKEN CFL CLEANUP

When a CFL bulb breaks, get everybody, pets included, out of the room and open as many windows as you can. Get a piece of cardboard for scooping, a glass jar with a metal lid, plastic bags for disposal, duct tape, and your vacuum cleaner. After 15 minutes, go back into the room. First scoop up the broken glass with the cardboard, carefully put it in the glass jar, and screw on the lid. If the bulb broke onto bedding, the compromised fabric should be placed in a garbage bag. For carpet, lift small glass fragments with duct tape, put the used tape in a plastic bag, and seal. Vacuum just the area where the mercury spilled, and remove the vacuum bag or empty the canister. Put the debris in a plastic bag. Label the jars and plastic bags with the contents. I would get them to my local recycling or household hazardous waste collection. Also follow these directions if you happen to break a mercury thermometer.

FIXING NOT REPLACING

It's always better to try to mend something than replace it. My husband, Jonah, the "Fix-It King" of our family, claims that I always *used* to say, "If it is broken, better throw it away!" It is true, I used to give up easily, simply because I didn't know how to fix anything and thought that it was too hard to learn.

The Fix-It King discovered that he could even fix cars. At the time, we were driving a vintage 1970 Mercury Cougar and had to keep it running since we had two little kids and lived out in the countryside. The mechanic's bills were draining the coffers, and so Jonah literally taught himself. He bought the mechanical car guide online and started doing our car repairs.

The rule in our family is to try to fix it before you ditch it! We have a basic fix-it kit in our house that gives us the equipment to deal with the basic household breakages and malfunctions. There are a few tools that should always reside in the house to deal with the small fixables, and they should be part of your fix-it kit (see below). If you don't have much of a budget for buying tools, check out your local flea market. There are usually very reasonably priced secondhand tools for sale. These tools often end up being worth the initial investment, and we use them all the time.

FIX-IT KIT

Exacto blade craft knife. A utility knife is very useful; get one with a retractable blade for safety.

Duct tape. Otherwise known as gaffer's tape, this durable tape was developed during WWII to seal ammo cases. It quickly earned a reputation for holding anything and everything together. It is cheap, strong, and versatile and there should be a roll (or two) in every house.

Tape measure. Get a metal retracting tape measure. This will last forever.

Extension cords. These are essential for working with electrical tools in far-flung parts of the house or yard. Make sure you get one with a three-pronged plug.

Flashlight. For illuminating the dark corners, basements, and crawl spaces.

Crescent wrench. An adjustable wrench for tightening or taking off nuts, tightening or loosening pipe connectors, and similar jobs.

Allen wrench. Also known as "hex keys," these come in graded sizes and are used to tighten bolts and screws with a hexagonal socket.

Hacksaw. A fine-toothed metal saw for cutting through screws, bolts, and other thin metal objects.

THE EASY FIX

It's a fact of life that things are always breaking or malfunctioning. Buying good-quality items means they'll last longer, but *nothing lasts forever!*

When you have a malfunction in your home, it will either be easy to fix or beyond your expertise. Don't try to fix things that you would regularly ask a professional to take care of. Apart from risking danger, you'll probably make things worse, which you'll have to pay the professional to sort out, too.

Here are a few fixes that even I have mastered.

CIRCUIT BOX AND CIRCUIT BREAKER KNOW-HOW

The circuit box distributes electrical power to the circuits in your house. When you open the box you will see rows of switches or, in older houses, screw-in fuses. Each circuit supplies power to a certain number of outlets and light fixtures or appliances. The circuit box also contains the main shutoff switch, which cuts power to all circuits. It is usually highly visible and is often larger than the others and colored red.

OVERLOADED CIRCUITS

In normal use, the switches or circuit breakers are in the "on" position. If a circuit has overloaded, the breaker will be tripped, and you can see that the position of the switch has moved to the "off" position or somewhere between "on" and "off." Switch it all the way to "off" and then back to "on." The circuit should function again normally. I recommend checking the appliance load on the circuit so it doesn't trip again. If the breaker feels loose when you switch it, you should get an electrician to come look at it. If your box has fuses instead of breaker switches, they will burn out and you'll be able to see that they need replacing. To change a fuse, first turn off the main shutoff switch as a safety precaution. (If it is nighttime, have a flashlight handy.) Make sure the new fuse has the same amperage as the old one.

CIRCUIT ID

Your circuit breakers should be labeled with the circuits they cover, such as "bedroom lights" or "kitchen lights." If your breakers aren't labeled, you can easily figure out what's what by getting a friend to help you identify the various circuits. Get your labeling equipment—a roll of masking tape and permanent marker will do—and then switch off your breakers one by one. Ask your friend to tell you where lights are going out. Once you've figured out the light circuits and labeled the breakers appropriately, move on to outlets and appliances. Circuits are not uniformly designed in all houses. It may take a while to figure out which circuits account for which outlets.

BASIC PLUMBING TIPS

The toilet and kitchen sink invariably start malfunctioning in the dead of night or on the weekend, when plumbers are twice as expensive to call. But these few tips will help you deal with minor problems or at least tide you over until you can get a professional to do a house call.

TOILET TROUBLE

If your toilet keeps running water after you flush, it is probably a problem with the ball stopper in the tank. To check for leakage from the tank, add a couple of drops of food coloring to the tank. Don't flush for a couple of hours, and if colored water appears in the toilet bowl, there is indeed a leak. Before you call a plumber, try this trick: turn the water off at the wall faucet and flush to empty the tank. Unhook the lift chain and check the ball stopper for damage. Scrub the interior of the tank with a kitchen scrubber to loosen any lime buildup. Then replace the ball stopper, reattach the lift chain, and turn the water back on. If the toilet still runs water, it's time to call the experts!

If your toilet is overflowing, there is probably a blockage. Use a plunger first, but if you can't unblock it after 30 plunges, try the snake instead. The snake is quite hard work and might take a while before you see results. Do persevere, though, because if the snake doesn't work, you'll have to call for the plumber.

SINKS AND BASINS

If your sink or basin is blocked, try the Drain Cleaner recipe earlier in this chapter (page 84). If that doesn't work, you'll want to try the plunger. If that doesn't work, it's time for the snake. Before you apply the snake to a sink, you'll have to remove the sink trap, which lies just below the drain. Sink traps generally unscrew; you can use your hands or pliers. If the trap is full of hairy goop, you have probably solved your problem. Wipe off the offending goop and replace the trap.

If your faucets are leaking, it is probably because the washers are worn out. It is not too difficult to replace washers if you have the right tools. First, you'll need to turn the water off at the wall and then turn the faucets on to get rid of any water lurking in your system. To take the faucet knobs off, you will need to unscrew them with a crescent wrench. Generally, the screw is hidden behind a concealing cap. When the faucet knob is removed, you'll see a six-sided nut, which you should unscrew. Underneath this nut is the valve. The washer is under the stem; so turn the stem upside down and take off the old washer. Take the old washers with you to the hardware store and make sure you get the right size replacements. The washer is on top of a "seat," which is a small brass disk. You should replace this at the same time, just to be on the safe side. If your faucet is still dripping after changing the washers, you should definitely replace the "seat," although not all seats are detachable. Barring that, as a fix, the next part to replace would be the valve stem. Again, take the old valve stem to the hardware store and make sure you get the right size replacement.

Another sink issue is a malfunctioning waste disposal unit. If you turn the unit on and nothing happens, listen for a pathetic groan or just silence. If it groans, there is something stuck in there. Silence is indicative of a more serious issue. Check to see if the unit has become unplugged, which sometimes happens, as the switch is generally under the sink and can easily and accidentally be switched off. Also check your electrical box to make sure the circuit hasn't tripped.

Make sure to check the reset button, usually on the underside of the garbage disposer itself, under the sink. Press the button and check to see if the disposer works.

For this next step, I urge utmost caution! If the disposer is still not working, turn off the main power and reach into the unit with your gloved hand, preferably with an implement such as long-handled tongs, to see if you can pull anything significant out.

If success evades you at this point, try using the disposer wrench. This wrench usually comes with the unit and fits into an indentation in the bottom of the disposal unit. If you don't have a disposer wrench, use an allen wrench (hex key) instead. If the wrench is able to moves the blades, it has worked. Remove the wrench, press the reset button again, and see if the disposer is operational. If the disposer wrench/allen wrench method doesn't work, make sure the power is switched off and stick a broom handle in the unit. Turn firmly until the unit starts to move. The broom method is your last resort. If the broom doesn't work after a couple of tries, it's time to call the plumber.

Please note that if you compost your food scraps and abandon your waste disposer you'll never have to deal with this kind of problem!

HOLE IN THE WALL

Small holes in a wall, like those from a nail or screw, can be easily filled with a smear of spackle. You can buy nontoxic spackle at the hardware store. If the hole is a few inches in diameter, you'll need to figure out whether the wall is made of drywall or plaster. If its drywall, you can use spackle for indentations up to 3 inches across. Apply the spackle with a putty knife as smoothly as possible, let it dry, and then sand it flush to the surface of the wall.

If the hole in the drywall is bigger, up to 10 inches, use webbing tape over the hole. Then apply a layer of joint compound or "mud" from your local hardware store, and let it dry. If the hole is still indented, add another layer of the mud and let it dry again. Now smooth on a layer of spackle and let it dry. Lastly, sand it down, prime it, and paint.

If you have a really big hole in drywall, it's best to cut the drywall back to the studs on either side of the hole to expose about an inch of the stud. You are going to screw a drywall patch to the studs. You can buy a sheet of inexpensive drywall from any building supply. Measure the hole and cut a piece of drywall that is slightly smaller then the area to be filled, ideally ¼ inch or less.

To cut drywall, you need to mark the line that you want to cut and then score a line about 1⁄16 inch deep through the drywall surface with an exacto blade. If you have scored well, the drywall will just break off along the line. Using drywall screws, attach the patch to the studs and fill in around the edges with joint compound. Cover the perimeter with drywall tape. Add another layer of joint compound over the tape and when the compound has dried, smooth over the spackle, sanding it when it dries. Paint first with primer and then paint to match the rest of the wall.

If you have a substantial hole in the plaster, you'll need to get patching plaster from the hardware store. Spray the hole with water to dampen the surface; this makes it easier for the new plaster to adhere to the wall. Fill the hole with a first layer, and score the surface with an old dinner fork. This allows the next layer of plaster to stick more easily. Apply another coat of plaster. When it has dried, smooth over with joint compound using a wide putty knife or a flat-sided piece of thick cardboard. When it is dry, sand the surface well and you are ready to prime and paint. You just saved a lot of cash!

WET CELL PHONE

It is a sad day when you drop your cell phone in water, especially tragic if you have important contacts stored inside. The most important step with a wet cell phone is to get it out of the water or other liquid as quickly as possible and remove the battery. Many circuits in the phone will survive if they are not connected to the power source.

If you have a SIM card in your phone, remove that, too. Dry the card and the battery with paper towel and set aside.

Next, dry the phone well, using a soft cloth or paper towel. Gently remove any water you can see. If you have a hair dryer, use it on the lowest setting to dry the phone further.

Get a plastic box with a lid, and if you have some silica packets (the kind you find in food packages to prevent moisture), put them inside with the phone for three days. Lacking silica packets, pour uncooked rice grains into the plastic box (a layer of approximately 2 inches), put the phone on top of the rice, then cover and leave for three days.

When you replace the SIM card and battery, it may well work! If your cell phone still doesn't work, plug the phone into the charger without the battery. If the phone works, you just need a new battery. Congrats!

REMOTE CONTROL REPAIR

If your remote control stops working, check the batteries. If the batteries are corroded in any way, that is probably the cause of the problem.

Clean off the battery contacts (those little springs) with a pencil eraser followed by a nail file. Make sure the contacts are in the correct position; if they are bent out of shape, bend them back. Replace the old batteries with new ones. If your remote is universal, it has the ability to be programmed to work with other devices. Consult the manual, or look the model up online. Check the instructions for reinitializing the remote; the codes may have become scrambled. Check the other components that you use the remote with. Unplug the television and DVD player, then plug them in again.

If the main issue with your remote is nonresponsive buttons, you may need to renovate the keypad. Loss of keypad conductivity is a big problem with remotes because the keys tend to lose their conductive paint with age. Look for a keypad repair kit. These kits are very affordable and will provide you with the conductive paint to make your keys responsive again.

FIXING CROCKERY

Accidents do happen and things get broken. In our house we get a lot of breakages in the kitchen due, in part, to the human dishwasher! If a plate, bowl, cup, or other piece of crockery breaks, you can try gluing it back together. If the item is in many pieces, it will be too laborious to glue and the results might not be great. One can always try to make an artful mosaic! If, however, there are only a few pieces, it is definitely worth trying to fix.

The best type of glue for crockery is an epoxy resin, available readily at the hardware store. Make sure your pieces are all clean and do a "dry run" to ensure that you really do have all the pieces of the plate or bowl. Note which pieces should be glued on first, so when you are gluing you aren't wasting time figuring which piece to attach next. Epoxy resin glue does not bond instantly, so you can make sure the pieces are fitting together perfectly. Apply glue carefully with a matchstick along the broken surfaces, and fit the pieces together. Wipe away any excess glue that seeps out of the join before it dries. This prevents glue lumps from hardening on the surface.

It is often a good idea to add some support to the fixed item while it is drying. Masking tape over the join works well for me, and rubber bands work great on odd shapes. Another option is to use a container full of builder's sand to support a glued item. I hear this works very well, but I'm wary of sand getting glued on. After a few hours, remove the support and you have fixed crockery.

SPLINTER FIX

Although we love our wood floors, they are susceptible to damage and splinters do occasionally form. It is best to fix a splintered floorboard sooner rather than later, as the splinter will ultimately detach from the board and get stuck in something, maybe even your foot! If you spot the splinter while it is just beginning, take a dab of wood glue and glue the splinter back down onto the floorboard. Wipe away any excess glue with a damp cloth and protect the repair with a sheet of newspaper; weigh it down—a book will do nicely. Let dry overnight, and in the morning lightly sand the spot so that the surface is smooth.

This method works well for other wood surfaces, too. If you lose the splinter, you'll need to use wood filler to repair. Clean the area and remove any paint in the immediate area. Fill the crevice or gap with the wood filler, making sure that there is a thin layer covering the immediate area around the damage. Leave overnight, then gently sand the surface smooth. Prime the area first if you plan to paint or varnish.

UNSTICKING DRAWERS

The drawers of newer furniture are often fitted with plastic or nylon runners and slides. These deteriorate easily, and parts often become detached. Take the drawer out of the chest and look at the slides on the sides or bottom. One may simply need screwing back into place. Look at the condition of the drawer itself; sometimes a nail or staple has worked itself out and consequently the drawer is slightly askew.

Wooden drawers are generally made from untreated wood, which is prone to swelling. If your wooden drawer is sticking, remove it from the chest and check the slides to make sure they are secure. Also check the drawer for loose nails or staples. The next step is to lubricate the slides and the bottom of the drawer with a dry bar of soap or a stick of beeswax. Use the plainest soap—nothing with extra moisturizer in it.

If this doesn't stop the drawer from sticking, you should sand the bottom of the drawer and the slides (if they are wooden). It is best to use a sanding block for this job to keep your sanding even. Wrap medium sandpaper (80–100 grit) around your block and gently sand. Check your progress frequently. As soon as the drawer opens and shuts easily, stop sanding and lubricate both the drawer bottom and the slides with a bar of soap or stick of beeswax. Now you can once again have access to your socks and hankies.

LAST BUT NOT LEAST—DUCT TAPE

As I've already confessed, I am not the Fix-It Queen. I just got lucky when I married the Fix-It King. However, our DIY monarch spends a lot of time out of town touring and can be gone for weeks at a time. In his absence, I keep duct tape close at hand. Even if I can't fix stuff, I can hold it together with duct tape.

Duct tape combines a cloth component with a very strong adhesive. It was first used during World War II to keep ammunition cases sealed and dry, and since then this heavy-duty adhesive tape has gone on to win many hearts and minds for its versatility and cheapness. Almost anything can be held together with duct tape: car doors, broken glass, plastic, tables, chair legs—you name it! Just make sure that whatever you want to tape is clean and dry. The tape can easily be torn along the cloth grain to make thinner strips to suit different applications. Use your imagination!

There are even a couple of medical uses: casts can be covered and protected by waterproof duct tape, and deep cuts have been successfully bandaged with duct tape. The duct tape treatment for plantar warts comes highly recommended: cover plantar warts with a piece of duct tape and leave it on for as long as the tape adheres. This won't survive a shower or a bath, so reapply a new piece of tape after bathing. The warts generally disappear in two to six weeks but sometimes sooner. This stuff is very nearly miraculous!

At home, we use duct tape to remove lint from clothes and furniture, for fixing vacuum hoses, mending guitar cases, covering holes in the soles of skateboarding shoes, and even repairing taillights on the car!

Duct tape is available in different colors these days, but even when it only came in silver or black it was very handy for making Halloween costumes, cardboard castles, and play houses. I've used silver duct tape to make a robot and a knight costume. The robot had a silver-taped cardboard box for the body and silver legs and feet made by taping over pairs of pants and shoes, capped off by a duct-taped box for the head. A knight's shield is really easy to make by taping over a cardboard cutout shield shape. The weapon of choice is created by carefully wrapping a cardboard sword cutout. This will delight your swashbuckling offspring.

Reinforcing books and binders is another handy use for this ubiquitous tape. There really is an inexhaustible list of possible applications—just make sure you have a couple of rolls. We even keep it in the car. One friend performed a temporary fix on his water hoses with duct tape. If in doubt, reach for the duct tape!

CHAPTER 5

Grow It: Get On My Land

Having a little patch of land is a beautiful thing. Whether you choose to cultivate or not, a little outdoor space is a luxury. For years, I felt that my lack of gardening experience was a drawback, but after I'd been given a mint plant that grew with a little watering and even less attention, I discovered that even I could garden.

I was also laboring under the misapprehension that I would need to make a significant investment in equipment to garden successfully, but I was wrong again. Apart from the most basic tools and some seeds, there is no major expense needed to start gardening.

Coupled with my complete lack of experience, I also felt that, as renters, we didn't want to put a lot of love and effort into a garden that we didn't own. I let go of that thinking when I visited my friend Eileen, who also rented but had a flourishing garden featuring vegetables, berry bushes, herbs, and flowers that she had brought with her from the garden at her last house. While this involved a lot of transplanting into pots, taking cuttings, and careful replanting, her backyard is divine. She feeds her family with her homegrown vegetables, fruit, berries, and herbs. She grows medicinal herbs and plants as well! If you have a deck, or even space on a fire escape, you too can get growing and create a garden with planters and window boxes.

BASIC GARDENING EQUIPMENT

All you need for tending a small garden is the barest minimum of tools. If you have a lot of land and weed clearing to do, you may need clippers or an electric trimmer, but before buying, check in with your neighbors or local tool-sharing organizations and equipment rental businesses. If you end up with branches in your garden waste, use them as a base for a freestanding compost pile (see below, page 122).

If you have a shovel, a pitchfork, a rake, a trowel, and some gardening gloves, you are well equipped. Certainly, a wheelbarrow, a hoe, and some good clippers will come in handy, but you can manage without them—people have grown gardens with far less. A variety of flowerpots, small cartons, and trays for germinating and seed starting will come in handy. These should be easy to get for free or very cheaply. I use all kinds of small plastic tubs for seedlings, and they work well. Instead of a wheelbarrow, I use an old laundry basket to cart the weeds and clippings to my compost pile. I employ a battered serving spoon as a trowel for planting seedlings. Garage sales and free lists often feature gardening equipment. New gardening tools are relatively inexpensive, so don't let yourself be deterred by setup costs. The only other expense you are likely to incur is the price of seeds or starter plants. Some vegetables can be grown from themselves, potatoes, for example, but more of that later.

When my kids were little, we would dig little patches and plant flower seeds, but the real agenda was playing. Instead of going out to the park we could just stay at home and play in the garden. We made a lot of temporary structures optimistically called "the fort" and "the castle." The garden at that time resembled a wild, forgotten place where all kinds of plants and weeds lived side by side. The rose bushes, planted long before we arrived, flourished unattended. In the spring the whole yard bloomed with sour grass, to the dismay of neighbors, who feared those pretty weeds migrating into their lawns.

I would complain to my gardener friends that I really needed to try my hand at gardening, coveting the delicate lettuces and tasty carrots they grew. Eileen, who ran a small landscape design business, explained to me that leaving my garden alone was good for it. Just "resting the soil" and then turning the soil over and tilling whatever is growing back under helps enrich it. If you want to get more proactive with soil enrichment, then try growing an annual grass-like crop such as barley or oats or leguminous plants like clover, vetch, peas, or fava beans, and then till the crop back into the earth.

COMPOSTING

The greatest free soil amendment of all is organic compost, which, with a little effort, you can provide for yourself. Whatever type of soil you have, you can greatly improve its quality by composting. If your soil is sandy, compost will help it retain moisture. If you have thick, claylike soil, the compost will help it drain. I was hesitant about composting, as I thought it required a costly composting receptacle. When I started reading up about composting, it seemed so scientific. Layering different types of compostable material, buying fertilizers to create the perfect composting environment, worrying about worm colonies, maintaining moisture levels—this all seemed too much for me to manage. Although there are some very nifty compost bins on the market, you can easily undertake composting without any special equipment or expenditure on your part. Compost for free!

COMPOST TEA

This liquid fertilizer lets you treat your whole garden to the benefits of your compost. It is easily assimilated by plants and soil in this form.

5-gallon bucket or similar container

aquarium water pump

water

compost food: 5 cups compost, 3 tablespoons molasses, 1 cup seaweed emulsion, 1000 mg Vitamin C or 2 tablespoons lemon juice

If you are using tap water, let it stand uncovered for 24 hours to allow the chlorine time to evaporate, as chlorine will kill the compost bacteria. Put the aquarium pump in the bucket and weigh it down so it doesn't rise to the top. Run the pump as the tap water is sitting, which will help outgas the chlorine. Then add the compost food; if you put it in a fabric bag you won't have to strain the tea to use in a spray bottle. Brew the compost tea for 24 hours, then turn the pump off and use the tea immediately. Dilute your tea with water using a ratio of 1:10. The beneficial bacteria will die quickly, so use it right away for maximum efficacy. Spray on leaves to protect them from disease, or drench the soil with this elixir.

TRENCH COMPOSTING

Before garbage collection, people did trench composting—it reduces trash and creates free fertilizer. Here is the easiest and cheapest way to create compost: all you need is a place to dig a hole and some kitchen scraps to bury in it. Dig a hole 15 inches deep and add 4 inches or so of kitchen compostables, then fill it in with earth. Do not use meat scraps (which will attract rodents), but everything else from the kitchen, including eggshells and coffee grounds, will work nicely.

This kind of composting takes very little effort, because your next step is to do nothing. Composting into the ground doesn't require any maintenance. You don't have to worry about keeping the compost moist or aerated; nature will just take care of itself. After a few months, you can dig into the hole, where you'll find rich compost that you can use to enrich other parts of your garden. I've also heard of digging shallow compost trenches between rows of plants, but I don't have enough space to really try it myself. With kitchen composting, chopping up the veggies makes for good compost; a handheld blender is great for this. The addition of paper makes for a good mix. If you have fears about rodents or a digging dog, you could place something heavy such as a few rocks or bricks on top of your pile.

In England, trench composting is often combined with a rotation of land use which helps maintain the soil's efficacy for growing vegetables. Divide a section of your garden into three areas: one for trench composting, the second leave fallow, and in the third, plant your vegetables. The following year, rotate the three areas. Where you were composting the first year, grow your vegetables; in the second, leave the vegetable patch to rest; and compost in the formerly fallow patch. You don't have to do it in any particular order, but if you keep rotating, you will maintain all areas nice and fertile.

I really recommend trench composting to novice gardeners because it works so well with such little effort. It is the lazy person's surefire way to great soil.

BUILDING A COMPOST BIN

My friend Chantal just made herself an affordable compost bin with 10 feet of rodent wire. Rodent wire is tough and has a small-gauge mesh: it provides a real challenge for rats and other unwanted "varmints." Chantal had the wire cut into two pieces—one 7 feet long and the remainder 3 feet. The long piece she rolled into a cylinder and attached the ends by tying them together with wire. The smaller piece became the base. She attached this piece to the cylinder with wire and turned up the edges of the bottom with pliers. This she placed on a few bricks with the addition of a lid to deter wildlife, and the bin was ready for filling. The lid can be made from a handy piece of plywood or anything else that would work.

The most important factors with a compost bin are adding the right kinds of compost material in the appropriate quantities and keeping the mixture moist. Compost bins get hot inside; the high temperature is crucial to the process. One way to nurture the heating process is to line your compost bin with a black garbage bag, opening up the bottom of the bag so the compost is sitting directly on the wire base. The garbage bag should be longer than the bin, so you can cover the top and seal the heat inside or open it up if things are getting too "ripe" inside. The ideal compost environment is composed of both nitrogen-producing materials and carbon producers. The ratio you want is one part nitrogen to three parts carbon. Nitrogen producers include veggie kitchen scraps (never meat or cooking oil), horse, goat, rabbit, or chicken manure, bone meal, blood meal, fish meal, garden trimmings, and weeds. Carbon-producing compost materials are straw, hay, dry leaves, shredded newspaper, brown bags, soiled food wrappings (not waxed paper), and cardboard. Sawdust or wood chips can be used in small portions. Build up layers by starting with a carbon mixture; bits of twigs and branches are good to help aerate the mix. Chop it all up if you have the time and the inclination. Next, add a layer of nitrogen-generating material, keeping in mind that the carbon layers should be three times the size of the nitrogen layers. If you live near the ocean and you can get kelp or seaweed, chop this up and add to your compost; it is very enriching.

Turn your compost over every week, using a pitchfork. Be thorough, moving the inner material to the outside and vice versa. Check that the compost isn't too dry or too wet. If it's too dry, add water sparingly. If the compost is soggy and smelly, leave it open to the sun and let it dry out.

FREESTANDING COMPOST PILE

To make a freestanding compost pile, follow the same directions as for the compost bin. Choose an out-of-the-way spot, preferably shady so that your compost doesn't dry out, and begin the pile with some carbon material such as small branches, wood chips, twigs, shredded cardboard, and the like. Make it at least 6 inches high. Then, add a layer of your garden waste and kitchen scraps. Some common kitchen compostables take a long time to break down—corncobs, banana skins, and orange peels will do better if they are chopped up. Finish with a layer of dry leaves. Turn the pile at least once a month, and make sure you cover the turned pile with dry leaves afterward. If you turn the pile weekly, it will process more quickly, but the schedule is entirely up to you. It's a good upper-body workout, if you look at it that way!

WORM COMPOST

Everything I read about worm composting made it sound too complicated for me. Hearing that worm compost can smell bad if the mix is wrong utterly deterred me. Then I spoke to my friend Maria, who grows vegetables in her backyard using soil made from worm compost. Despite the potential downside, she had decided to go ahead and try it anyway. She took an old plastic garbage bin, drilled holes in the sides, and started her compost with a layer of cut-up cardboard and old newspaper. She then added a layer of wood chip mulch, then some kitchen scraps, and a box of live worms that she bought at a gardening supply store. She adds kitchen compostables three times a week and, once a week, a little more shredded paper and mulch. Maria's advice was to make sure the compost is kept moist and aerated. Her trick was to turn it once a week when checking the moisture level. When your compost is a brown, crumbly humus, it is ready to use. Maria shovels out a few loads of compost, sifts the worms out, and throws the worms back in the bin. The compost bin has a heavy lid (a piece of wood with a weight on top), and she hasn't had any problems with rodents, large or small. As for the dreaded bad smell, Maria said it only developed when she left the compost unattended for a few weeks. She noted that it was easily rectified by adding more mulch.

USES FOR COMPOST

Compost is like a vitamin B shot for your garden, and whichever way you make it, your garden will love you for it. It is worth checking at your local dump for free compost; if your area has a green bin program, chances are they will have free compost available. Compost is the best amendment to enrich the existing soil in beds. You should add up to 30 percent compost and dig it into the top layer of soil. Our local "HANC" recycling center has all fruit and leaf compost that smells lovely. They get the fruit from a smoothie stand!

Compost is an excellent addition to give a boost to plants that have been moved and are consequently a little traumatized. Also, use compost in your potting mix for seedlings and starters. Again, a 30 percent ratio of compost to the soil is best.

Use your compost as mulch for an effective weed control. A layer of compost on your soil also helps conserve moisture in the ground, vital in these times of multiyear droughts. Compost will fertilize and help deter weeds. If weeds are a serious problem in your garden, try laying newspaper sheets on the soil with a thick layer of compost over the top. The newspaper will inhibit the weed growth.

One woman filled 5-gallon plastic buckets halfway with food scraps. She placed soil directly on top of the compostables and planted some flower seeds. She wrote that they were the prettiest and most abundant flowers she had ever grown! More conventionally, even a little compost at the bottom of a hole dug for planting will encourage a plant's roots to grow downward to seek out the nutrients. Green is good!

PLANTING TIME

Don't get discouraged by the overwhelming and often contradictory advice in gardening books and guides. The whole process seems complicated when you approach it mostly through the literature. Talk to neighbors who have green thumbs. People who work at gardening centers are always generous with free wisdom. The season in which you start your vegetable and herb garden dictates what you should plant. Figure out which plants are easiest to grow at the appropriate time of year. The better results you get from your crop, the more you will be encouraged to keep gardening. Learn as you grow.

Some plants do best when germinated indoors and transplanted as established seedlings. Germination time varies from seed to seed, but most will germinate within six to 20 days. Plant your seeds in trays, cardboard egg boxes, or small plastic pots. If your pots are recycled containers, make sure to perforate the bottoms. The little pots made of peat which can be planted directly into the ground are great and relatively inexpensive, making the transplant easy. Use a pasteurized soil medium or planting mix as a clean soil to help the seeds get established. Make sure your seeds are kept warm, place them in good light, and keep them moist. It's always a good idea to make labels for the seeds. Before transplanting the seedlings, take them outside in the daytime and bring them back inside at night for a few days; this will help acclimatize your baby plants to the outdoors environment. Follow the instructions on your seed packets to make sure you are seasonally correct with your planting. Most importantly, remember to water as directed.

KEEPING YOUR GARDEN GREEN

- Plant some bamboo. Bamboo contributes to the balancing of oxygen and carbon dioxide in the atmosphere.
- Don't use a leaf blower. Compost instead, and never burn leaves!
- Plant a garden using xeriscaping—no water needed. www.xeriscape.org
- Capture rainwater for gardens.
- Fertilize with grass clippings.
- When watering your garden, turn on the water early in the morning to minimize evaporation.
- Try not to fertilize before a storm to avoid the fertilizer being washed away.

- Protect young seedlings from cold weather, heavy rain, and hungry critters by reusing plastic milk and juice jugs; cut off the bottoms and place the jugs over the seedlings. When the plant is grown you can recycle the jug.
- Introduce ladybugs to your garden; you can buy them at the gardening supply store, and they will happily eat destructive aphids.
- Plant marigolds to discourage beetles.
- To kill slugs, dig a shallow hole in the soil and place a bowl in it so the edge is flush with the surface of the soil. Fill the bowl with beer or a mixture of water, sugar, and yeast. The slugs will come to drink and end up drowning.
- Leave a corner in your garden with a few logs, or just long grasses, providing a habitat for beneficial wildlife like ladybugs and birds.
- Use recycled materials to build raised beds, glass frames, and other garden structures.

PLANNING YOUR VEGETABLE PATCH

Vegetables love the sun. Make sure your veggie patch gets good sunlight. Avoid any trees with big root systems close by, as they tend to suck up all the water. If the land runs east to west, plant taller plants such as corn on the north side so they won't block the sunlight for the shorter plants. Plant rows 10 to 20 inches apart. Growing herbs and vegetables together is smart: the herbs deter insects, as do pretty marigolds, which can also make a beautiful garden border.

In front of the tallest crops, plant the bigger vegetables like potatoes and cabbage; these two will grow well next to each other. In the front of the patch, plant the smaller vegetables, bordering everything with the herbs. Herbs need less water and will get less at the edge of the beds.

Start your garden with a few different vegetables and see what grows best for you. Some vegetables combine well in rows; spinach and carrots are a good example. Spinach grows quickly and can be done in about six weeks, making way for your carrots to come through. Lettuces and radishes also grow well together. Once your plants are in the ground make sure to keep them watered and weeded. Be sure to check for damage from insects or other nibblers.

My advice is to make your garden as simple as possible to begin with. Plant only a few easy-to-grow vegetables to encourage yourself and branch out into more variety when you feel confident and have gained some practical knowledge. This winter, I will only plant carrots, spinach, kale, potatoes, and turnips; this is enough for me to handle. I know that carrots take longer to germinate, so I will take care to keep them watered, sowing the spinach with them, as I suggested previously. As with all autumn vegetables, the carrot seeds will go in a couple of weeks before the first frost. Frost information for your particular area is easy to find online, or check the venerable *Farmers' Almanac*.

For my kale, I germinate the seeds in little pots and then separate the seedlings and plant them a couple of inches apart in the soil. I do this so they won't grow in clumps and compete with each other too much. You have to give them room to grow.

I am going to plant organic potatoes and turnips that have sprouted as starters. This has worked really well in my patch already, so I'm doing it again.

MOON GARDENING

Lunar gardening or moon gardening uses the wisdom of ancient farmers preserved in old sayings like *Plant when the moon is growing full.* Just as the moon controls the ocean tides, it also influences groundwater tables and the movements of fluids in plants, called geotropism. The old wisdom to plant as the moon becomes full follows the logic that the seedlings get the benefit of the moisture brought to the surface by the gravitational pull of the moon.

The best time to turn over soil is in the last quarter of the moon, when the water tables are at their lowest point, as it is easier to turn over dry soil than wet soil. Also, weeds are less likely to grow back at this time due to the dry conditions.

For in-depth lunar garden logic, read *R J Harris's Moon Gardening*, by R J Harris and Will Summers.

HOW TO GROW TOMATOES FROM SEEDS

FOR SEEDLINGS:

Soilless potting soil, small pots, tomato seeds, and recycled plastic produce bags

FOR GARDEN:

black plastic, mulch, and stakes or other supports

GERMINATION

When you are planting seeds, don't overcrowd them; they need room to flourish. As soon as the true leaves emerge (see below), the seedlings need to be transplanted—ideally to containers at least 4 inches deep, giving the roots room to grow. To avoid the potential weed seeds and diseases that soil often contains, use a soilless potting mix, which is primarily sphagnum peat moss. Don't pack too much potting soil in the containers; fill about two-thirds. Hand-sift the potting mix to remove lumps and add water so that it is moist but not wet. (Note that some seeds such as parsley or lavender might need soaking or chilling, so check the seed packet for special directions.)

Plant approximately three seeds in each container, sprinkling the small seeds on the surface but sticking larger seeds under the surface. Cover the small seeds with a little more potting mix and water again. Likewise, give the larger seeds a little more water, too.

Make your own mini-greenhouse by putting the seedling containers in a plastic bag or under a sheet of plastic. Make sure that air can get in and circulate to avoid mold issues. A good spot for germinating seedlings is on top of the fridge—seeds like a warm, draftless environment.

The first two leaves that emerge are actually *cotyledons*, part of the seed itself. When the true leaves emerge, remove the seedlings from plastic and put them in direct sunlight or under a fluorescent grow light for 12 to 18 hours a day, keeping them moist and warm. When the true leaves appear, it's time to give the potting soil some nutrients, so add a little fertilizer to the pots.

If more than one seedling has germinated in a pot, either separate the seedlings into different pots or remove all except the strongest seedling. Hard to do, I know!

HOW DOES YOUR GARDEN GROW?

While the plants are gaining strength indoors, prepare the garden bed by preheating the soil where the tomatoes will be planted. Simply lay down some black plastic to heat up the soil; our tomatoes just love a nice warm bed. When you are getting close to transplanting your tomatoes, start introducing your tender plants to their new environment gradually. Leave the plants outside in their pots for a few hours a day, increasing their time outdoors incrementally. If the weather turns bad, bring the pots back inside to protect the young plants.

When your tomato plants are fully acclimatized to the outdoors, you are ready to plant. My trick is to transplant in the cool of the morning or late afternoon, not during the heat of the day. You will avoid wilting this way. Plant them a foot apart, leaving room for air to circulate and to prevent insects from clustering. Bury the plants deep, leaving only a few leaves above the surface. Tomatoes will grow roots all along their stems, and planting deep like this ensures that the root system of the plant will be good and strong. Stick your stakes or tomato towers into the soil at this point to avoid damaging the roots by inserting them later. You don't have to buy stakes from the gardening store—any sticks will do. Recycle and reuse what you have at home before buying more.

Keep the plants well watered once they have been transplanted. When the weather turns warmer, add mulch to your tomato patch—mulch will help keep vital moisture in the soil. Never mulch before the sunny weather arrives, as it will cool down the soil.

Water tomato plants often and thoroughly in the beginning. Once the fruit begins to ripen, water a little less to concentrate the sugars in the fruit. Don't let them go thirsty, though. If the plant wilts, it will drop both its blossom and fruit.

GROW YOUR OWN ALOE VERA

It is great to have an aloe plant that you can harvest a stem from when somebody gets a burn, sunburn, or starts to itch from a stinging plant or insect bite. If you live in a warm climate you can grow an aloe plant outdoors in full sun; just choose soil that drains well. Water your aloe regularly but wait until the soil looks dry before rewatering. Aloe has a hard time surviving a frost, so if your climate is colder, grow your aloe plant indoors. Find a window spot where it will get as much sun as possible. The aloe's root system is shallow and spreading, so use a wide planting pot rather than a deep one; make sure the pot has good drainage holes. Aloe propagates through baby plants that grow on the outside of the mother plant. Gently remove a baby stem from the mother plant and repot; it will soon flourish with regular watering.

To harvest aloe, cut a stem with a sharp knife and either squeeze the sap out or cut the stem to expose the interior and scoop the sap out. Apply directly to sunburns and itchy, irritated, or dry skin. Heating aloe in the oven and then laying the warmed stem, sap side down, on sore muscles feels great too!

GROWING LETTUCE

There are two general types of lettuce: "head" lettuce, which refers to those that grow into a discernable head, and "leaf" lettuce, which doesn't form a head. Leaf lettuces are also known as "cut and come again," which refers to harvesting—outer leaves can be picked and the inner leaves continue to grow.

Lettuce is a cool-weather crop, and despite its fragile leaves and delicate flavor, it is easy to grow even for the novice gardener. In North America, lettuce crops do well in the spring in both northern and southern regions. Fall is the preferred second lettuce season for northern states, while winter is best for southern states.

Lettuce seeds can be sown directly into the garden bed, but some gardeners prefer to germinate them indoors for extra sturdiness. This works particularly well for "head" varieties like romaine, butter, and iceberg.

To germinate seeds indoors, use potting mix and sow seeds onto the surface of the container. Lettuce seeds need light to germinate, thus you should not cover these seeds with potting mix. Keep them warm in a sunny window spot or an enclosed porch. Keep the potting mix moist with frequent waterings. When the seedlings are a couple of inches tall, you can thin them out, if need be. Start to "harden" them by gradually exposing them to the outdoors environment. Take the seedlings outside for a few hours a day if the weather is moderate. If the weather turns colder, don't leave them out overnight. After a couple of weeks of acclimatizing, your lettuce seedlings should be ready to transplant. Lettuces like cool weather and moist soil that drains well. Try to do your transplanting on a temperate, cloudy day; if it's hot, wait to transplant in the evening. Stagger the planting of lettuce seedlings by planting a small row every two weeks; this way you will be able to harvest continually throughout the season and have a full salad bowl at all times!

If your lettuce seeds are going straight into the garden, do wait until the frosts are over. Densely sow the seeds in a sunny spot, and thin out your seedlings when they are about 3 inches tall. Cover the seeds with a very thin layer of loose soil, but don't bury them, as they need light to germinate. Sow in rows 10 inches apart, always remembering to stagger the planting so that you get a continuous crop; also keep them well watered and weeded. The secret to growing lettuce is plentiful and frequent watering.

Harvest "head" varieties when they are big enough for you to use. Cut the head at the base, leaving the stem and root intact, and in time you should get a second head of lettuce. With "leaf" varieties, harvest gradually, starting with the outer leaves; the inner leaves will continue to grow and can be picked later. Hence the popular name for these lettuces, "cut and come again."

THE CARE AND FEEDING OF LETTUCE

The biggest problem with growing lettuces, apart from vagaries in the weather, is that slugs love them. Other insects are also keen on the tender leaves, but slugs really do search them out. I don't recommend using pesticides or insecticides for any plants, especially leafy greens, but luckily there are nontoxic pest deterrents. Try laying a boundary made of sand (slugs hate coarse textures), crushed eggshells, or coffee grounds. If you have a rabbit population, you will need to cover your lettuces with wire netting.

TATERS, TURNIPS AND RUTABAGAS

Potatoes, turnips, and rutabagas are all relatively easy root crops to grow in a home garden. All three can grow in containers, too. Container-grown root crops just need a deep enough pot to allow the roots to roam.

POTATOES

Leave a couple of potatoes in a warm spot—I use my kitchen vegetable basket. Let a potato sprout and develop "eyes." Cut this "seed potato" into cubes that have one or two eyes each. If you are "seeding" little potatoes, just plant them whole.

The best time to plant potatoes is when you know that there won't be any frost during the growing time; potatoes take two to three months to mature. An early spring planting and a late summer planting works here in my Northern California garden. Potatoes like full sun and rich, moist soil.

If, like me, you have limited space to grow, a potato mound is a good alternative to planting rows. To make a mound, designate a 4-foot-diameter area and dig deep. You want to put the compost beneath the roots so that it can feed them. Create a raised mound, at least 10 inches high, and plant about six seed potatoes in your mound. When the potato sprouts are about 10 inches tall, "hill" more soil around them to halfway up the stem. This will keep the potatoes growing under the surface of the mound. If the potatoes push up to the surface, they will grow green, which makes them inedible. Keep hilling the growing sprouts until they start to flower, always keeping them well watered.

If you have room for rows, make them 3 feet apart and allow 10 inches between plants. Dig the trench for planting about 8 inches deep and fill the trench only halfway with soil. When the potato sprouts emerge after a few weeks, add soil to fill in the trench. When the sprouts get to be around 10 inches tall, "hill" again halfway up the stem. If you want tender, sweet-tasting baby potatoes, plant them 5 inches apart and harvest early after flowering.

Harvest your potatoes two or three weeks after the plants have stopped flowering. Gently loosen the soil and pull out the potatoes. If the weather is warm and dry, lay the unwashed tubers on the soil and leave to dry for a few days. If the weather isn't so great, take the tubers to a warm, dry, and ventilated space. Basements or garages are great for the drying of potatoes. If potatoes have been properly dried, usually a three-day process, they will keep in a cool dark sack for three to six months.

If you are going to grow potatoes year after year, you should rotate the growing area. In this way, you'll avoid exhausting the soil, and escape diseases and insect infestations.

TERRIFIC TURNIPS AND REMARKABLE RUTABAGA

I was extremely happy when I realized that the "swede" I had grown up with in England was alive and well here in America. Here it is commonly known as rutabaga.

Both turnips and rutabaga can be planted in spring and fall. Both of these root stocks like cool weather, so the spring planting should be early and the greens should be harvested in early summer. Plant in rows 20 inches apart in an area that gets full sun. Turnips should start growing 6 inches apart from each other, while rutabagas like a little more room and should be 8 inches apart. Both types of seed should be planted in a half inch of soil and watered well to ensure germination.

When turnips are 4 inches tall, thin them out so they are 4 inches apart. With rutabagas, thin them when they are 2 inches tall to a distance of 6 inches apart. Cook the greens from the plants you have removed; they will be sweet and tender. Turnips will be ready to harvest in two months. Never let them get too big because they taste "woody." Try to harvest turnips when they are the size of a handball. Rutabagas need three months to mature, and grow best in cool weather; therefore, the fall crop is usually the best for this root veggie. The spring crop should be harvested in early summer before it gets too hot. Remember to eat the tasty greens too!

PARSLEY, SAGE, ROSEMARY, AND THYME: KITCHEN HERB GARDEN

You can plant herbs with your vegetables to deter some insects. Rosemary, sage, mint, chives, and marigold flowers are particularly beneficial in this way. Herbs need less watering and can happily grow at the edges of your garden. A dedicated herb garden is a very good thing, too. Most herbs can grow in pots, either inside or outside, whichever is easier for you. Prolific characters such as mint are often grown in containers to stop them from taking over the entire garden. Some herbs prefer full sunlight—basil, chives, dill, oregano, rosemary, tarragon, and thyme; while mint and chervil like a little more shade. Plant your seedlings accordingly, either by starting the germination process in pots indoors or by sowing them directly into the ground. Cilantro and dill do not transplant easily, so it is best to sow them where they will be growing. Mint and rosemary grow easily from cuttings, and thyme can be divided by cutting off one root tendril from an existing plant and planting the tendril.

The great thing about growing herbs is their immense usefulness combined with tenacity. Many are really low maintenance and need very little time and attention. Just start growing the herbs that you use the most. You'll greatly enjoy harvesting from your own garden instead of at the supermarket!

Here are directions for getting your herb garden populated with some classics.

SUPER SAGE

Sage grows well from seeds or cuttings. Sow seeds thinly in potting mix, either indoors or outdoors under glass until germination. Indoor seedlings should be transplanted when they are 2 inches high. Be warned: one sage plant can cover

3 feet. Containers are a good option for keeping this herb manageable. Water moderately, as sage is pretty robust and will take care of itself. I would even go so far as to say it thrives on neglect! Harvest sage leaves before the plant blooms. To dry the leaves, hang them in bundles and keep in a dry and well-ventilated place. Simply store in an airtight container and enjoy in soups and suppers for months to come.

AWESOME OREGANO

Sow oregano seeds indoors in little seed pots, beginning after the last frost. Set the seedlings in a sunny window until they germinate: this will take about a week. Transplant when the seedlings are a couple of inches high. Make sure the frost is over—oregano seedlings won't survive extreme cold. Oregano will grow in any soil but prefers a dry environment, so water very sparingly unless the weather is extremely dry. When oregano begins to flower, pinch off the buds; this will make the plant grow bushy and improves the flavor of the leaves. Start harvesting when the oregano plant has reached 4 inches in height. Pick your leaves in the early morning because when the sun comes up it will dry the oil in the leaves, giving the herb its distinctive flavor. You can use oregano either fresh or dried. To dry, hang in bunches in a dry, well-ventilated area and then store in an airtight container.

SUPERB CILANTRO

Cilantro grows and goes to seed really quickly. So, if you want to keep a continuous supply coming, it's a good idea to plant every three to four weeks to keep your crop going. Plant cilantro seeds ¼ inch deep and 2 inches apart in an area that gets both sun and shade, preferably morning sun and afternoon shade. Spring and fall are the best seasons to grow cilantro; the summer is just too hot for it. (Cilantro will go to seed fast if the weather is really hot.) When the cilantro starts to flower, pinch off the buds to make the leaves grow. Cilantro should be harvested in eight weeks. Pick the outer leaves first to encourage the inner leaves to keep growing. Dried cilantro doesn't have such a strong flavor, so this herb is best used fresh.

CHEERY CHIVES

Chives are hardy and easy to please. They love rich composted soil but will grow happily in the garden or in a container filled with potting compost. Chives are a diminutive member of the onion family, and the whole plant—flowers, leaves, and root bulbs—can be eaten. The flowers are also very pretty. Grow chives from seeds indoors in the springtime. Sow seeds in little pots filled with potting compost, and keep them growing inside until they are a month old, then transfer to the garden. Plant chives 6 inches apart in a spot where they'll get either full or partial sun. As I mentioned, chives don't need a lot of attention; just water them moderately. If you are growing chives purely for eating, pinch off the flowers when they appear. Chive flowers are pretty in a salad, so maybe you'll decide to let some plants flower and keep others just for their leaves and bulbs. Cut the leaves from the outside of the plant with scissors and always leave 2 inches at the bottom of the leaves. Chives will grow well in a container filled with potting compost, indoors or out—just keep it moist and chives will flourish. Chives propagate quickly, so you can dig up the chive plants growing outside during springtime and divide up the bulbs, replanting the bulbs close to the surface for your next crop. Chives do lose flavor when they are dried, so I recommend just using them fresh.

PERFECT PARSLEY

I always thought that parsley would be the easiest of herbs to grow. Guess again! It is actually the most challenging of the herbs I've grown, though your experience may be different. The germination period is rather long, up to a month in a warm, sunny room. Parsley prefers rich soil, which means that a container filled with potting compost is an easy way to create a good home for this herb if your garden soil isn't especially rich. Sow generously in potted compost and keep moist and well drained. Thin out all the small seedlings and concentrate on the strongest ones.

Harvest parsley by leaving 2 inches at the bottom of the stems. This will encourage new growth. Parsley is very nutritious, brimming with Vitamin C, but drying decreases nutrients, so I prefer to use my parsley fresh. If you want to dry parsley, hang it in bunches in a cool, ventilated space. Store the leaves in an airtight container. The stems can be composted.

BOUNTIFUL BASIL

Basil is a sweet and pungent member of the mint family. This lovely herb grows year round indoors and will also flourish in the summertime outdoors. Basil loves the sun and generous watering. Germinate basil seeds indoors in a potting mix, keeping it moist and in a warm, sunny window spot. Transplant the basil seedlings outside in the spring after the last frost. For indoors, grow it in 8-inch pots or containers filled with potting mix. Make sure your young basil gets as much sunlight daily as possible. Feed your indoor basil plants with fertilizer monthly; if the leaves are pale it is undernourished. Outside, a sunny spot and daily watering will keep basil happy and burgeoning. Indoors, aphids can be a problem; in your outdoor herb garden, slugs are the culprits. Spray an indoor aphid infestation with nonpetroleum dishwashing liquid. Put

1 teaspoon in a spray bottle and fill with water. Never use an insecticide on a plant you intend to eat! Protect basil from slugs by encircling each plant with wood ash, sand, crushed eggshells, or coffee grounds.

When transplanting basil seedlings, wait until they are 6 inches tall and space them 10 inches apart in the soil, as they have a propensity to bush out. They are ready to harvest or transplant when they are 6 inches tall. Pinch off any flowers immediately and harvest leaves from the top. To harvest a bunch big enough for making fresh pesto, cut off the top few inches of your most robust plant.

If you want to dry basil, cut with the stem still on and hang in bunches in a dry, dark, ventilated space. When dry, remove the leaves and store in an airtight container. Chuck the stems in your compost!

TOP-NOTCH THYME

Thyme is a hardy herb—it pretty much will grow itself once established. It prefers dry and sunny conditions but will weather the winter outdoors unless it's freezing cold. It grows well from cuttings or you can germinate seeds indoors in potting mix; the seeds will germinate in three or four weeks if kept on a warm sunny windowsill. When seedlings are 4 inches tall, transplant to the garden after the last frost in spring. Thyme grows prolifically and can be quite pretty in a flower bed. It is a honey bee attractor, as well. Thyme needs very little of your time!

It is so easy to grow an abundance of thyme that when midsummer comes, you can harvest a lot and dry it for teas and tincture, as well as for cooking. Thyme is indicated medicinally for coughs and colds, upset tummies, and diarrhea. It makes a great antibacterial mouthwash and preventive for lice and crabs.

Dry thyme in the customary fashion by hanging it in bunches in a dry, dark, well-ventilated space. When dry, flake the leaves off the stems and store in an airtight container. To make thyme tea for a cough or upset tummy, just add a teaspoon of dried thyme to boiled water and add honey to taste.

Make mouthwash by adding a teaspoon of thyme tincture to a cup of warm water. For unwanted guests such as lice and crabs, add a teaspoon of thyme tincture to ¼ cup of olive oil, and comb infested hair with a comb dipped in the thyme-infused oil; repeat as needed.

THYME TINCTURE

large glass jar with a tight-fitting lid
1 cup packed dried thyme
2 cups apple cider vinegar
dark glass jar for storage
cheesecloth

Combine thyme and apple cider vinegar in a jar, and seal.

Shake every day for a month, and then drain the liquid through cheesecloth or muslin.

Store the tincture in dark glass and put the thyme leaves in your compost.

Use tincture diluted with water for a mouthwash. For a medicinal tea, add a teaspoon of tincture to hot water and add honey to taste. Only drink 2 cups of thyme tea daily from dried herbs, fresh herbs, or tincture for best results.

RESPLENDENT ROSEMARY

Rosemary is an easy plant to grow once it is established, but it is difficult to start from seed. I suggest growing from a cutting—once in the ground, the rosemary pretty much grows itself. If you are growing in a container, choose a large pot with good drainage. Feed rosemary with compost tea or fertilizer every month for best results. Bring pots indoors before the first frost. Outdoor rosemary will weather the winter well enough, but this herb loves warm, dry weather the most. It does well in full sun or in partial shade and doesn't need watering unless it is visibly wilting. Pinch off the aromatic needles and use them fresh in your food dishes. Rosemary is also a great medicinal herb; use dried rosemary to make a tea to relieve cramps, muscle aches, and upset tummy. Rosemary is said to be a good rejuvenator for after illness; it comes recommended as a memory stimulant, as well. Use dried rosemary as an infusion, simply adding it to hot water to make a steam, or adding dried or fresh rosemary to your bath. Relax and remember the good things in life.

LUXURIOUS LAVENDER

Lavender is not a fussy plant; it will tolerate most soil types and grows quickly from cuttings, which is how I advise you to cultivate this sweet-smelling herb. Seed germination is laborious—these are fragile seedlings, and germination time is around a month. Lavender bushes generally last five seasons before thinning. Lavender needs full sun to really flourish.

Plant your cuttings after the last frost in the spring or in early fall, at least two months before the frost sets in. Prune your lavender back every year after it has bloomed. Harvest the lovely lavender flowers after the plant has bloomed, cutting the stems in the morning before the sun dries the flowers out. Dry your lavender by hanging it in long-stemmed bunches or by laying it on a screen in a dark space.

LAVENDER TINCTURE, TEA, AND INFUSION

Lavender is prolific—in a couple of seasons you may well have flourishing bushes. In addition to using the flowers in potpourri, bath salts, lavender sachet bags, and recipes, it is easy to make a tincture of lavender. A tincture is easy to make with the dried flowers, and tea and infusions are even easier.

To make a tea, add 1 tablespoon of dried lavender flowers to 1 cup of boiling water. Good complementary herbs to add would be yarrow, chamomile, or St.-John's-wort—a teaspoon of any of these will make a nice therapeutic brew. Lavender tea helps relieve headaches, insomnia, depression, upset tummy, and gas, and also has a general calming effect both physically and mentally.

To infuse lavender, add 1 tablespoon of dried flowers to a bowl of boiling water, drape a towel over your head, and breathe in the soothing vapors. The infusion works well for headaches and nervous tension; it also provides relief for colds and cough. As a steam, lavender is pure bliss!

The tincture is a good way to take lavender for all the above complaints, ensuring a therapeutic effect. Take a teaspoon of tincture in hot water with honey to taste. Use this tincture for cuts. Simply rub the tincture neat onto a wound to ease discomfort, to disinfect, and to minimize scarring. Tincture can also be used to treat skin problems like acne and eczema.

LAVENDER TINCTURE

quart jar
dried lavender flowers
1 cup clear alcohol such as vodka
2 cups filtered water
dark glass jar for storage
cheesecloth for draining

Fill a clean quart jar halfway with dried lavender and pour in the vodka. Add the filtered water and screw the lid on tightly. Now give the mixture a good shake. Store the jar in a cupboard where its cool and dark, shake once or twice daily for a month. Strain through muslin or cheesecloth into a dark glass jar and screw the lid on tightly. Discard the lavender heads in your compost.

AMBIENT GARDENING

Even if you are not actively gardening, you can still reap the benefits of a wild backyard. Rocket, sorrel, purslane, and dandelion leaves are easily found and foraged; just wash them and add to your salad. Purslane is very high in omega-3 fatty acids and has a tangy, lemony taste. This superfood grows everywhere and is commonly considered a weed by gardeners!

BLACKBERRIES

Although blackberry bushes are not loved for their thorny brambles, this plant has been used and revered for centuries. In Europe, the blackberry was considered a charm against evil spells and is used to treat diarrhea, hemorrhoids, ulcers, burns, sore throats, fevers, colds, and the flu. It's also used as an energy stimulant, especially when recuperating. Blackberry is very astringent, owing to high levels of tannin. Tannin is medicinal, particularly for upset tummy complaints. Ancient Greeks used blackberry for gout and Native Americans used it for all of the above; they also harvested the young shoots for salad and made a tough twine out of the stems.

Blackberries are amazing; packed with vitamins A, C, and E, they rate high in antioxidants. They're also a good source of magnesium and potassium and brim with fiber—7 grams in 1 cup of raw berries. They are really easy to cultivate, so if you have a garden, they are probably already growing there. If not, a magnificent bush will start happily from a cutting, with very little encouragement. If you're not growing berries yourself, you'll be able to harvest them from roadsides, parks, and vacant lots. Blackberry bushes are sturdy and prolific, and you'll find them anywhere and everywhere. Below are a few tips and some recipes to show just how versatile blackberries are.

TIPS FOR PICKING

Take the kids—they love blackberry picking! Only pick firm blackberries. If you pick them red, they'll stay unripe, and don't pick overripe berries, which taste bad. Try not to squash berries in your container, because they will deteriorate more quickly; only go a couple of inches deep. Don't wash berries until just before you use them; they will last longer unwashed. Keep berries in the fridge or somewhere dark and cool.

FREEZING

Store-bought blackberries are expensive, so freeze some berries for making desserts and smoothies when the season is over. For best results, wash and hull the berries. Freeze them in small batches in ziplock bags, removing as much air from the bag as possible. Now you can bake blackberry-apple cobbler affordably year round.

BLACKBERRY LEAF TEA AND BLACKBERRY ROOT TEA

Like all berry leaf teas, blackberry is supportive of reproductive health, especially for women. It is also great for upset tummy and diarrhea. Pick the leaves and dry them outdoors in strong sunlight. Store the dried leaves whole in an airtight container. Use a mortar and pestle to grind the leaves when you want to make tea; 2 teaspoons per cup is suggested. Steep for 5–10 minutes before serving. This tea is very palatable, and your kids will love it with a little honey.

Blackberry root tea makes a stronger decoction than the leaf tea. This helpmeet was used to treat dysentery during the Civil War. The most astringent part of the blackberry is the root, so take the root of a young blackberry cane and boil it gently until the liquid reduces. Dilute the decoction in equal amounts water and use it for intestinal upsets, hemorrhoids, and to support a cold or the flu. It doesn't taste as good as the leaf tea, so it's best just for adults. Undiluted, the decoction can be used topically with a compress for burns, or to treat ulcers and sore throat. A free medicine that grows by the side of the road!

BLACKBERRY CORDIAL

Blackberry cordial can be made with or without alcohol; either way it is a great tonic for a cold or flu and stimulates energy. Wash and hull berries, and using a sieve, gently press berries to yield juice. For every quart of juice, add ½ teaspoon of cloves, ½ teaspoon of nutmeg, and 2 pounds of sugar. You can use less sugar to taste, or substitute ⅔ cup of honey for every cup of sugar. If you use honey, the cordial will have to be stored in the refrigerator, while the sugar-based version can live in a cupboard.

Gently boil the juice, spices, and sweetener for 5–6 minutes. Skim off any foam that forms. Remove from heat and let cool.

When the mixture is cool, pour it into sterile glass bottles and seal tightly.

If you want to add alcohol, a good brandy will work nicely; add whatever amount you prefer. Berry bracing!

BLACKBERRY VINEGAR

Blackberry vinegar can also be used medicinally. Diluted in water, it can reduce a fever, help with coughs and colds, and ease upset tummies. It is a beloved traditional condiment in England, poured over apple pie and cream!

Steep washed and hulled blackberries in malt vinegar for three days.

Strain the liquid. Add 1 pound of sugar for every 2 cups of vinegar. Boil gently for 5 minutes, skimming off any foam that forms. Allow to cool.

Bottle in a sterile glass container and seal tightly.

INDOOR GARDENING

Even if you don't have any outdoor space you can still grow some of your food in the house. Growing herbs in the kitchen is easy to do and will save you money. Chives, mint, oregano, parsley, cilantro, and basil all do well indoors so long as they get good sunlight.

You can buy starter plants or start herbs from seeds. For planting indoors, use a mix of equal parts potting soil, sand, and peat moss or humus. Six-inch pots are good for the root length of most herbs. You can expect to be able to harvest parsley, cilantro, and chives 12 weeks after starting the seedlings. Herbs should be watered moderately; they don't like to be too wet. Also, feed them with organic fish emulsion once a week when they are growing. Cilantro, watercress, and dill are short-lived, so keep starting new seedlings. They won't produce seeds indoors, so if you want to keep a supply going, you'll have to buy your seed stock. Thyme does well in a pot indoors, as do rosemary and oregano. Never harvest your herbs too heavily; by taking a few leaves at a time as you need them, the plant will continue to thrive.

Without getting into hydroponics and growing under artificial light, there aren't too many indoor opportunities for growing food. Radishes and short-rooted carrots grow well indoors in containers. Both are gratifyingly quick-growing crops, and they make great projects for kids. Plant radish or carrot seeds in 8-inch pots and cover with ¼ inch of potting soil. Place a piece of glass or plastic wrap over the pot to conserve moisture while you are waiting for the seeds to germinate. Set in a sunny window spot and keep the soil moist; the veggies should be ready to eat in six weeks or less.

THE ACE SPROUTING METHOD

My friend Ace got us started on sprouting a few years ago. He was inspired by an old friend of his parents whom he hadn't seen for years. When he and the long-lost pal reconnected, the friend had renamed himself "Sprouts" and was spreading the word on sprouting! Ace caught the bug and, like Sprouts, began taking sprouting projects into the local schools and proselytizing to all his friends. I now consider sprouting to be "growing food." Make sure you source good seeds, certified organic if possible, so you can know that they haven't been treated with any chemicals.

Sprouts are a truly great source of antioxidants, vitamins, trace minerals, amino acids, protein, and phytochemicals. Talk about a superfood! Cruciferous sprouts such as cauliflower and broccoli are strongly indicated for prostate health. Diets high in cruciferous sprouts have been shown to reduce levels of lung, breast, colon, and ovarian cancer. Sprouts take three to five days to grow to edibility, with a twice daily rinsing and draining schedule. You can make sprouts from seeds, beans, grains, and nuts.

Choose from:

Seeds: alfalfa, clover, radish, flax, broccoli, sunflower
Beans: mung, lentils, garbanzo
Grains: rye or wheat berries
Nuts: almonds or hazelnuts

There are many more possibilities but this is a good basic list.

If you are using seeds, start with a couple of tablespoons' worth to see how many you use. When you are choosing a jar for sprouting, pick one with plenty of space for the sprouts to grow into, as they will get significantly bigger. I use a quart-size mason jar, which is plenty tall enough.

The first thing to do is pick through your seeds, beans, and grains. Put them on a large plate or baking dish and compost anything damaged or abnormal looking. Look for and remove any small stones or dirt. Rinse the sorted stock and place in a jar or bowl. Cover the seeds with a couple of inches of water. I suggest you use filtered or spring water to get the best-quality sprouts.

Plunger. To unblock stubborn sink drains and toilets.

Drain "snake." Basically a metal cable that you wind down into sink drains to loosen, break up, and push through blockages.

Screwdrivers. Phillips screwdrivers are a must—keep both a large and a small one to deal with different-size crosshead screws. You'll also need flat-blade screwdrivers for use with other types of screws.

Pliers. A tool for gripping objects firmly. Blunt-nosed pliers are for electrical work, gripping, and cutting wire. Needlenose pliers are great for gripping awkward objects, often too small for hands to get to.

Wire strippers. These are special scissors for stripping the plastic casing that electrical wire is bundled in.

Hammer. For banging in nails and all kinds of things!

Chisel. For chipping away at things that need to be removed.

Drill. A tool for drilling holes; drills usually come with an assortment of different-sized drill bits.

Magic can. Keep a can or box for all stray and reusable nails, nuts, screws, bolts, washers, and other bits and pieces.

Soak seeds overnight, roughly 12 hours. Beans can soak for an extended 24 hours, but I do get good results soaking both mung and garbanzo beans overnight.

After the soak, the seeds or beans need to be strained. I have a small-gauge screen, sold for sprouting jars, that fits onto the rim of a quart-size mason jar. Another perfectly good way to create a strainer on your sprouting jar is to use cheesecloth and secure it tightly with a rubber band or two. Turn your sprouting jar upside down and let the soak water drain out. Some people like to leave their jars inverted to ensure complete drainage. If you choose to do this, place the jar upside down on a dish or pan.

The sprouts need to be watered and drained morning and night for the next three to five days. After a few days you will see the sprout shoots growing. Just taste them to see if they are ready—they will be soft but firm and sweet-tasting. As a rule of thumb, they are ready when the shoots are around 2 inches long. To harvest, just give the sprouts one more rinse and then store them in an airtight container in the fridge.

SPROUTING TIPS

Try to remember to pour off the soak water into a pan and feed this protein-rich water to your plants. They will thank you by thriving! When you figure out how many sprouts you use in a week, you can set your sprouting schedule so you always have fresh sprouts for eating. I try to start a second jar on the third or fourth day after the previous batch.

COMMUNITY GARDENS

Another way to garden is to join or start a community garden. Community gardens are created on both public and privately owned land, mostly on vacant lots in cities, and provide plots where you can grow vegetables, herbs, and flowers. They sometimes include a community-worked project such as an orchard. In Europe, local councils provide allotments—plots of land for gardening. There, the system is well established, but even in the United States most cities do have a community garden program and you can apply for a plot. I've heard that while the waiting lists can be discouragingly long, plots are often allocated far more quickly than you've been led to expect.

The history of community gardens in the Americas has its roots in the government-sponsored "relief gardens" which began during the Great Depression. "Victory gardens" were established during World War II, and the 1970s saw an upswing in urban gardening and the creation of community gardens. That impetus is alive and well today. The American Community Garden Association is the best resource for locating projects in your area, and they also offer advice on setting up gardens.

If you can't find a community garden to join, look around for somewhere to start one. If you find some vacant land that looks like it could be cleared, find out who owns it. The Tax Assessor's office at your local city hall will know who it belongs to if all else fails. Any land that you want to garden on needs to have a water supply, so the next step is to find out if there is an existing water hookup that can be activated and metered. Contact your local water authority and ask them to do a site investigation. If no water has been supplied to the site, find out if they will lay in a lateral line from the street main.

Once you have found out if a garden is feasible on the lot, contact the owner and see if he or she will lease it for use as a community garden. The lease can include a "hold harmless" clause to protect the owner from any liability claims. You can also have the gardeners sign individual waivers regarding liability issues. These kinds of community gardens are temporary by nature, but try to get the longest lease you can. A community garden is enriching for everybody who participates, and it draws neighbors together. There is no doubt that a lot of work and planning goes into these projects, so having a good group of people to work with will really help.

A less organized form of the community approach is garden sharing, where people who want to garden use gardens that aren't being cultivated. I've read about garden sharing where the gardener(s) and the owner share the produce; but there are no hard and fast rules. Get creative!

GUERILLA GARDENING

Another form of gardening that is characterized by a lack of rules is guerilla gardening. Popularized by Richard Reynolds in South London, his brand of guerilla gardening is about reclaiming neglected land and beautifying it by creating a garden. Reynolds cites the 17th-century Diggers, who grew food on common land, the Zapatista agricultural movement in Mexico, and the MST (Movement of Landless Rural Workers) in Brazil as the inspiration for his singular style of gardening. Guerilla gardeners don't look for permission from landowners; they just go ahead and start gardening, mostly at night! The Green Guerillas started guerilla gardening in New York City in the early 70s, petitioning the city to turn the abandoned plot they had transformed at Bowery and Houston into an official community garden.

If you fancy a spot for guerilla gardening, check out the guerilla gardening website (guerrillagardening.org) for some inspirational posts and photos. The website encourages Guerrilla gardeners to be friendly and cooperative with the local community and law enforcement. This is a most genteel revolution in land use! The first step is to identify your neglected land and figure out what kinds of plants would work well there. Enlisting friends lets you have more fun and garden quickly before attracting any unwanted attention. When the planting is done, consider how you will tend the garden; you will have to bring water if there is none, and keep the area weeded. Guerrilla gardeners also use seed "bombs," made of packed soil and seeds, which they throw onto neglected land that is difficult to reach.

My friend Annie and her neighbors started a guerrilla gardening initiative in her neighborhood recently. (In the process, Annie placated her husband, who was yearning for a garden.) They reclaimed a strip of urban land that had become an eyesore for the locals. The land flanks a freeway off-ramp and was a home base for sorry characters who lived in the debris of trash, discarded car batteries, and used needles. Annie was inspired by a random planting of a cherry tree, which looked alone in the wasteland.

Without engaging in any bureaucratic process, Annie started to solicit free plants online and got a great response from local gardeners. Through flyers, e-mail, and word of mouth, Annie got the word out to her neighbors that she needed help clearing the land, and people showed up on the designated day and started to dig. Annie is at pains to point out that she isn't an expert gardener, but she knew enough to bring in free compost from the dump and plant an ornamental garden, as the land was too contaminated to risk growing vegetables. In a few months, she has transformed an ugly, sad patch of land into an amazing flower and shrub garden, creating a gardening community. Unfortunately, the land is owned by the local transportation company, and they have liability issues. The future of the garden is not certain, but for now it is beautiful and healing to anyone who sees it. Because many guerrilla gardens on municipal or corporate land do gain official status, we have crossed our fingers and signed petitions, hoping this little garden can survive.

CHAPTER 6

Eat, Drink, and Be Merry

For me, the heart of a home is the kitchen. I spend a lot of time in this room every day preparing our food, doing dishes, paying bills, and socializing. Even though my kitchen is not very big, it is the busiest room in the house. In the winter, it's the warmest room in the house, and year round it's the most relaxed. Viv, my youngest son, sits at the kitchen table and does his home work while I cook supper. This is what I call multitasking: peeling potatoes and helping with algebra. If friends pop by for a visit, we invariably sit in the kitchen and have a cup of tea; on Pizza Friday, every chair is taken and extras are brought in from the garden.

To be healthy, we have to enjoy the process of shopping and preparing good, wholesome food. The more cooking and baking you do, the more time you'll be spending in your kitchen. You'll save a lot of time "to-ing and fro-ing" when you organize your equipment and supplies so that everything is easy to reach. I firmly believe that the family or household should eat a meal together every day if possible. A meal is not just about nourishment; it is also the meeting place for those who live together to check in with each other and share the stories of the day.

Some of my earliest memories are of helping my mum in the kitchen: rolling out pastry, shelling beans, or licking out the icing bowl! I also vividly remember shopping with her; she always bought vegetables in season and knew exactly what cuts she wanted from the butcher. When she worked in the town, she would shop daily for fresh provisions. I now see how attentive she was to the fine details of feeding us the best food that she could afford. From her, I learned that sacrificing quality for a low price is a false economy. She scrutinized fruit and vegetables, never bought cheap cuts of meat, and considered dessert a treat, not a daily event.

Our food sustains us and also has the power to heal us. In the last 30 or so years, there has been an increased awareness of not only how foods affect us, but how we are affecting food. We know that processed and fast foods are nutritionally inferior to fresh, whole foods, and we know that pesticides and processing chemicals degrade the quality of the food. The argument continues to rage whether GMOs (genetically modified organisms) are beneficial to us and our environment. In the meantime, I avoid them and hope that the original seed stock of the planet can retain its integrity while we figure out whether scientific augmentation is beneficial. The unprecedented rise in the incidence of degenerative diseases, allergies, and obesity since this unofficial experiment on our food began leads many of us to reject mainstream thinking. Eating well and having the vitality to lead our lives is our birthright. For me, this means promoting a fresh whole foods agenda for my family.

It doesn't matter how little experience you have with cooking; it isn't rocket science, and you'll improve with experience. Don't be daunted by the first section here, which explains bread, yogurt, jam, and pickle making—you can master them all!

The recipes in this chapter are all tried and tested many times over, and

I can vouch for them all to be affordable and yummy. Many of my family's favorite dishes we've learned to make from our friends, so don't be bashful—when you love a dish, ask for the recipe!

BREAD IS LOVE: BAKING IT

There is nothing more scrumptious than the smell of freshly baked bread in your kitchen. While bread is not hard to make, it does take a little time and practice. Making bread with commercially bought yeast is easier and less of a commitment timewise than the bread I make with a sourdough starter, but I urge you to try making your own starter and discover, as I did, how delicious, nutritious, and inexpensive your homemade loaves will be! Buying commercial yeast is a continual expense and adds a good percentage of cost to your loaf. If you cultivate your own starter, the cost of a loaf is:

flour—50 cents
salt—5 cents
olive oil—35 cents
sugar—25 cents
Add it up—only $1.15 a loaf!

SOURDOUGH STARTER

A starter is a batter made of flour and water in which wild yeast grows. As your container for the starter, use a wide-mouthed mason jar, an old mayonnaise jar, a large pickle jar, or a stoneware crock—use plastic only as a last resort. Make sure that the jar you choose is large enough for the starter to double in size.

With a wooden spoon (metal inhibits wild yeast), mix together 1 cup of plain flour and 1 cup of spring or filtered water. Don't use tap water, because the chemicals in it will inhibit the yeast growth. Pour this starter mix into your jar, cover loosely with a clean kitchen towel, and let stand in a warm place. Leave a little breathing room in the jar; don't fill it to the brim.

It will take a few days, usually two to five, for the starter to mature. When it is bubbly and smells pleasantly sour, it is ready. Stir it well, and put the lid on it. If you are using an old mayo or pickle jar, perforate the lid with a hole for ventilation.

Refrigerate. Once the starter is in the fridge, it needs to be "fed" every week or two.

FEEDING YOUR BREAD STARTER

Combine one part starter, one part filtered water, and 1 cup of flour. Mix with a wooden spoon and add to starter.

Stand starter in a warm place, covered loosely, for one day before returning it to the fridge.

If you aren't making bread every week and begin to accumulate a lot of starter in your fridge, either compost it or, better yet, pass it on to friends with instructions for how to feed the starter.

PROOFING YOUR STARTER

The starter will take a while to proof; this can vary from 1 hour to 8 hours or even longer, depending on your altitude and the air temperature. I suggest starting the proofing the night before you plan to bake your bread.

Pour your refrigerated starter into a large glass or plastic bowl. Wash out the starter jar with boiling water to prevent anything unwanted from growing in there.

Add 1 cup of warm filtered water and 1 cup of flour to the bowl, and stir with a wooden spoon. Leave it sitting in a warm place for a few hours.

When the starter looks bubbly, with a frothy surface and a pleasant sour smell, it is ready to use.

SOURDOUGH BREAD

2 cups proofed starter (any extra starter should be poured back into your clean starter jar, freshened with flour and water, and left in a warm place for a day before returning to the fridge)
3 cups flour (preferably unbleached, but any will do)
2 tablespoons olive oil
4 teaspoons sugar
2 teaspoons salt

In a bowl, mix the olive oil, salt, and sugar into the starter, and then add the flour 1 cup at a time. Knead until a soft dough forms. I knead by hand, but you can use an electric mixer or food processor.

Transfer the bread dough to a large oiled bowl. Cover it with a towel and let it rise in a warm place until it has doubled in size. The dough has risen when you can poke a finger in it and the hole doesn't close up. The rising process might take up to 10 to 12 hours.

Punch the dough down with your fists and knead it back into a ball. Form the dough ball into a loaf shape and put it on a baking sheet. Dust it with cornmeal or lightly grease it with olive oil. Cover with a kitchen towel and let the loaf double in size again.

Preheat oven to 450°F (230°C). Pour an inch of water in a roasting pan and place it in the bottom of the oven. Put your loaf in a floured and oiled pan or on a pizza stone preheated for 30 minutes in the oven. If you want a split-top loaf, make a lengthwise gash in the top of the loaf with a sharp knife. Brush the loaf with water and bake it for 15 minutes. During this initial baking period, mist the oven with water using a spray bottle. This misting will give you a nice, firm crust.

After 15 minutes, remove the pan of water and reduce the temperature to 375°F (190°C). Bake for another 40 minutes.

When you tap the bottom of the loaf and it sounds hollow, it is baked. Cool on a rack and enjoy your homemade bread.

Breadmaking is a lot of work to start with, but it's worth persevering. Your technique will refine, and then you can begin making all sorts of variations on your basic loaf. If you have doubts or any troubles the first few times, just remember that the ingredients are all very affordable and that sometime soon you'll be eating the most delicious homemade bread for pennies! This is the way our forebears made bread for centuries, so you, too, can master the technique.

MAKING YOGURT

Yogurt is a great, kid-friendly source of natural probiotics, an integral part of a healthy diet. Eating live-culture yogurt helps maintain the balance of micro-flora in the intestines, bolsters the immune system, and alleviates food allergies. I always thought yogurt making would be too precise and complicated for me, and then I found this simple method, which yields 12 6-ounce yogurts from $5 worth of ingredients. This makes it affordable to eat yogurt every day. Just add fresh fruit or honey, or both, if you fancy!

SUPER SIMPLE YOGURT

1 gallon whole or low-fat milk
1 small container (8 ounces) plain, unsweetened live yogurt
cooler, regular size, big enough for a few pitchers and 12 small jars
kitchen thermometer
3 plastic pitchers, quart-size mason jars, or large drink bottles
12 small glass jars or ceramic pots with lids

Sterilize the 12 jars or pots that the yogurt will be decanted into by pouring boiling water into them and letting them sit for 5 minutes. Empty the water out.

Heat the milk in a large saucepan over low heat on the stove top, stirring gently. When the milk reaches 170°F (76°C), turn off the heat and continue to stir for a few minutes to make sure the milk doesn't stick to the bottom of the pan and burn.

When the milk has cooled to 105–110°F (40–43°C), mix up the yogurt so it's smooth and add it to the milk. Stir the yogurt in well; this inoculates the milk with the yogurt culture. For best results, make sure the yogurt is fully dissolved in the milk.

Pour the milk mixture into the 12 sterilized jars and place them in the cooler. Fill the three pitchers with hot water from the tap, place them in the cooler next to the yogurt, and close the lid.

Leave the cooler in one place without moving it. The fermentation process will take 4 to 8 hours. If you are concerned that the temperature in the cooler is low, you can refill the pitchers with hot water midway through. Be sure to keep the lid closed as much as possible while you are reheating the pitchers.

When the yogurts are set, a clear yellow liquid will form on the top of the yogurt—this is called *whey*. You can either stir it back into the yogurt or pour it out; whey is rich in protein, so I prefer to stir it in. Put the lids on the jars and store them in the fridge.

If you want to use one of these yogurts as the starter for your next batch, use it in the first week; otherwise freeze it and thaw before using.

LIVE-CULTURE PICKLING

Pickles are great tasting and really good for you. Fermented foods are natural probiotics and integral to good digestive health. Don't be intimidated; making pickles is not difficult, and you don't need any expensive equipment, either. When I make pickles I don't seal the jars, because this kills the live culture in the pickles. Instead, I keep opened jars of pickles in the fridge. The list of pickleable foods is pretty long and includes nuts, all sorts of vegetables, beets, turnips, brussel sprouts, cauliflower, and even fruit. Pickled apples are an old favorite. Start by pickling the vegetables that respond most easily to the process: cabbage, radishes, carrots, and onions. You can add all kinds of herbs and spices to your pickles, to your family's taste.

EASY-PEASY SAUERKRAUT

1 head green or red cabbage, chopped however you like, fine or coarse. For every cup of cabbage add:

1 tablespoon umeboshi vinegar (Japanese plum vinegar, found at Asian and health food stores; if you can't get it, substitute apple cider vinegar, malt vinegar, or distilled vinegar)

1 tablespoon brown rice vinegar (you can substitute any of the above vinegars for this Japanese vinegar)

1 tablespoon mirin (optional; Japanese rice wine for cooking, available at Asian and health food stores)

Toss the cabbage with the vinegars in a large bowl. Press a plate that fits snugly in the bowl down over the cabbage, and place a clean weight on top. Give the plate a little pressure every time you think about it.

After a few hours the pickled cabbage will be ready to eat. To yield the greatest flavor results, I give it 24 hours to ferment.

If the kraut tastes too salty, then just rinse it before serving. This sauerkraut will last in the fridge for three to five days.

If you use any of the substitute vinegars (distilled, apple cider, or malt vinegar), experiment to see if you like the taste. Make a batch with just one or two cups of cabbage until you get your variation right!

ENGLISH PICKLED ONIONS

These were my favorite as a child, and I remember getting scolded for drinking the pickling juice, which is actually a really healthful elixir! This is close to the way my grandma made pickled onions—just the way I like them, crunchy and strong!

pickling onions or shallots
malt vinegar (or vinegar of your choice)
sea salt
filtered water
pickling spices: a generous pinch of coriander seeds, cumin seeds, black peppercorns, juniper berries, allspice, mace, cinnamon—any combination or all

To prepare the onions or shallots, soak them for a bit in a little warm water; the outer skins will come off much more easily. Cut off the tops and bottoms, making sure each one is in perfect condition, as any spoilage will compromise the pickling process.

To make the brine, dissolve 8 ounces of sea salt in 2 quarts of water, stirring over low heat. Place the onions in a bowl and submerge them in the brine. Invert a plate over the onions, and place a weight on the plate. Leave the pickles for two days on your kitchen countertop, making sure the brine is covering the onions.

Drain off the brine, pat the onions dry, and pack them into clean, sterilized jars. Fill with vinegar and pickling spices. Seal jars tightly and store them in a dark cupboard—they will last for at least a year. After you open a jar, you should refrigerate it.

SANDORKRAUT'S SERIOUS SAUERKRAUT

Live-culture foods give our digestion a huge helping hand, and making your own sauerkraut is cheap and easy. This recipe from the fermentation master, Sandor Ellix Katz, is the best basic recipe. When you have mastered it, you can experiment with pickling all sorts of vegetables with this method.

a large ceramic crock or food-grade plastic bucket
a plate that fits snugly inside the crock/bucket
a clean weight (such as a glass gallon jug filled with water)
5 pounds cabbage
3 tablespoons sea salt

Chop or grate the cabbage. I prefer to waste nothing and chop the "heart," or core, too. Scrape chopped cabbage into a large bowl and sprinkle salt on it as you go.

Pack the salted cabbage in the crock, a little at a time, tamping it down firmly with a utensil (a nonmetal spatula is good).

Cover the cabbage with the plate, making sure it fits snugly. Place a clean weight (the water-filled jug) on top of the plate. Your goal is to submerge the cabbage under the brine. Apply pressure every few hours during the first day. If there is not enough brine to rise above the plate, add salt water (1 teaspoon salt to 1 cup of water, stirred to dissolve). Cover the crock with a towel to keep the dust out.

Leave the cabbage to ferment and turn into sauerkraut. A corner of the kitchen is fine. For a slower fermentation, place the crock in a cool, out-of-the-way spot such as a basement or the back of a kitchen cupboard. Check the sauerkraut every two days; if mold appears, scoop it off. This is only a surface phenomenon; the sauerkraut itself is protected by the brine.

After five or six days, taste-test your the sauerkraut and decide if it is ready. Take out a jar or two of the sauerkraut and keep it in the fridge. Repack your kraut crock carefully, making sure the plate and weight are clean and that there is plenty of brine to cover the kraut.

Always start a new batch before your old one is finished. You can use the remains to enrich the new batch.

MAKING JAM

There are a few rules to observe when making jam or canning fruits and vegetables, but don't let the process intimidate you. You have to begin with clean, sterilized jars, and you have to boil the sealed jars after packing them.

Sterilize the jars simply by washing them well and placing them in the oven at 200°F for an hour. Don't preheat the oven; let the jars and the oven heat up together. Another method is to run the jars through the dishwasher on the hot cycle. The best tried-and-true "old school" method is to boil them in a canning kettle, making sure that the water covers the jars by at least an inch.

The jars are not the only things that need to be sterilized—you also have to sterilize the jar lids and rings in boiling water. A crucial utensil is a pair of jar tongs, which make lifting jars out of boiling water possible. A canning kettle, which comes with a canning rack for the jars to rest on, is the best way to process jars using the water bath method. You could use a large stockpot with a wire rack placed inside, but a canning kettle is far superior and will make things much easier for you.

Traditional jam recipes are always heavy with sugar and rely on pectin for good results. I prefer to make jam really simply using just fruit, water, sugar, and lemon juice.

SIMPLE BLACKBERRY, RASPBERRY, OR STRAWBERRY JAM

2 cups blackberries or raspberries
2 cups sugar
2 teaspoons lemon juice
1 strand of lemon rind
optional: an apple slice
equipment: water bath, jars with lids, tongs

Crush the berries with a potato masher, but not too hard. Put all the ingredients in a stockpot and boil over high heat for 5 minutes, stirring the mixture to prevent it from sticking or burning. Reduce the heat to medium-high and continue to boil and stir. Remove any foam with a large spoon. (I use this foam as a flavoring for cheesecake, a flavored whipped cream icing, or something else yummy.)

After a while, usually half an hour, the jam will begin to thicken up. You can put it in the fridge to speed up the process; test the readiness by lifting a spoonful and seeing if it sets. If your jam doesn't thicken, you can add a little more lemon juice or a slice or two of apple. Pectin, which is regularly used to thicken jams and jellies, is made from apples. Thus, a slice of apple will serve the same purpose.

When the jam is ready, pour it into sterilized jars. The jars should be warm when the jam is added, so keep the sterilized articles in the oven, dishwasher, or canning water bath until you need them; ditto the lids and rings. Make sure to leave a generous ½-inch gap between the jam and the top of the jar—this is known as headspace in the world of jam. Place lids on the jars and screw them on firmly.

Place the sealed jars into the water bath and cover with at least an inch of water. Boil for 10 minutes. Using jar tongs, lift the jars and let them cool at room temperature. You will hear the lids seal when they make a popping noise as the domed lid is sucked down.

Processed jam will last at least a year and makes a lovely gift. For small batches you can make your jam and store it in the fridge as soon as it has cooled off. If you freeze berries, you can defrost them and make jam whenever you need it.

CANNING VEGETABLES AND FRUITS

Canning or "putting up" is an old-fashioned way of preserving food. If you are a gardener with a prodigious harvest, this is an excellent option for you to consider. Apples are easy to can and they work well in pies and to make applesauce. Fruits, vegetables, soups, stocks, and much more can be canned. Follow the directions below to can not only apples but green beans, carrots, corn, and other fruits such as peaches and pears.

CANNED APPLES

Wash, peel, core, and slice your apples. Put them in a pot and cover with water. Bring them to a brisk boil and boil for 5 minutes.

Spoon apple slices into warm, sterilized jars and pour in some of the cooking liquid, leaving ½ inch of headspace. Seal the jars with sterilized lids and rings.

Submerge the jars in a water bath, covering jars with at least an inch of water. Boil for 20 minutes. Remove the jars with jar tongs and allow to cool at room temperature.

MAKE IT—REALLY GOOD RECIPES

SOUPS

Soup is great served for lunch or dinner. We often have a light supper of soup, bread, and salad. My kids like to have rice added to their soup if they are extra hungry.

MISO SOUP

This traditional Japanese soup is a big favorite. Miso is a staple of the macrobiotic tradition, too. The fermented soy bean paste is beneficial to your intestinal flora and is also considered an anticancer food.

2-inch piece dried kombu seaweed
1 quart water, or more
½ block tofu, or more
2 carrots
a few shiitake mushrooms, fresh or dried
2-3 leaves leafy greens, washed and shredded
2–3 scallions
3–4 tablespoons miso paste (red or white)

3 ounces soba noodles (optional)
dried nori (seaweed) strips (optional)
tamari or soy sauce (optional)

Place kombu and water in a pot. Bring to a boil and simmer for 5 minutes.

Chop tofu, carrots, shiitakes (already soaked and soft if dried), and greens. Chop scallions separately. I chop everything finely when I'm making this for kids. Add these ingredients, except the onions, to the kombu pot. Bring to a boil and reduce to a simmer again.

If you want to make the miso heartier, cook soba noodles in a separate pot. Remember to run cold water over them when you drain them, otherwise they continue cooking.

Remove the soup pot from heat and add miso paste. It's important not to boil miso, as it loses its goodness and flavor. To dissolve the miso paste easily, take some of the soup stock and stir it into the miso, then return it to the soup.

Add optional strips of dried nori and cooked soba noodles. Garnish with chopped scallions.

I add a little tamari or soy sauce if I feel the soup needs more "heat." You can also add more miso paste if the soup tastes "thin." Once you have made miso soup a couple of times you'll get your quantities adapted to your taste. Even if you only have miso paste and a block of tofu you can make a miso soup, so don't worry if you don't have the right vegetables—just use whatever you have!

SIMPLE BEAN SOUP

Follow this simple recipe and substitute any vegetables you have—squash, peppers, turnips, parsnips, broccoli, literally any veggie will work. I often blend bean soups, as they give a smooth creamy texture, which is very kid-friendly.

6–8 ounces dried beans (use any variety: black, navy, pinto)
3 cups water
1 potato, chopped
1 carrot, chopped
chopped garlic to taste
1 ounce butter or 3 tablespoons oil
1 onion, chopped
1 teaspoon yeast extract (Marmite) dissolved in 2 cups water or 1 vegetable stock cube dissolved in 2 cups water
salt and pepper, to taste
herbs of choice (oregano, dill, thyme, or other)
1 cup plain unsweetened yogurt or ½ cup sour cream (optional)

Soak beans overnight in cold water. Drain.

Place beans and water in a pot and bring to a boil. Add the potato, carrot, and garlic. Simmer for 1 hour.

While the beans are cooking, melt the butter in a skillet and sauté the chopped onions until they're soft and transparent.

When the beans are soft, add the yeast extract or vegetable stock.

Add the onions. At this point you can put the beans and veggies in a blender, if you so choose. Add seasoning to taste and garnish with chopped herbs.

If you want to make the soup creamier, remove from heat and gently stir in yogurt or sour cream.

SIMPLE SEASONAL VEGETABLE SOUP

This is the method I use for any kind of vegetable soup.

1 big onion, chopped
1 big potato, chopped
carrots, parsnips, or any other vegetables in season that you fancy, chopped
1 cup red lentils
2 ounces butter or margarine or 4 tablespoons olive oil
6 cups water, or more
2 tablespoons tomato paste (optional)
1 teaspoon yeast extract (Marmite), or dissolved vegetable stock cube
1 bay leaf (optional)
1–2 cloves garlic, chopped (optional)
salt and pepper
1 cup plain unsweetened yogurt or ½ cup sour cream (optional)

Bring lentils to a boil in 6 cups of water. Reduce heat and simmer the lentils for 20 minutes or so until they are soft. Reserve cooking liquid.

While the lentils are cooking, sauté the onion in butter or oil in a skillet until soft and transparent. Add the rest of the chopped vegetables and optional chopped garlic and sauté for 5 minutes or so, making sure to stir.

Put veggies, cooked lentils, reserved cooking liquid, yeast extract, bay leaf, and optional tomato paste in a large stock pot. Add another cup of water, and stir to combine. Simmer for about an hour. Add seasoning to taste. Remove the bay leaf.

Serve with your homemade bread and a dollop of your homemade yogurt!

CHICKEN SOUP

Make the Stock

1 whole organic chicken or 2 pounds chicken with bones (I use whatever is left of a roast chicken and add some extra chicken thighs if there isn't enough meat.)
1 big onion, coarsely chopped
1 carrot, coarsely chopped
2 celery stalks, coarsely chopped
4 quarts water
salt and pepper, to taste

Place the chicken and chopped onion in a stockpot with the water and bring to a boil. Reduce heat and simmer for 2–3 hours. Two hours is fine, but more is better; the longer you cook it, the richer the stock will be. When I was cooking for a dear friend who was extremely ill, a Chinese herbalist told me to cook down the bones until they dissolved, as this releases the healing marrow into the stock.

Remove stock from heat and take out the chicken. Allow the bones to cool, then pick off all the meat and reserve it for the soup.

When the stock has cooled, the fat will harden on top. You can just remove this and discard it. Stock can be saved in the fridge or freezer and used for future soup making.

Make the Soup

½ pound cooked chicken
chicken stock to cover (dilute with water if you need more)
1 onion, chopped

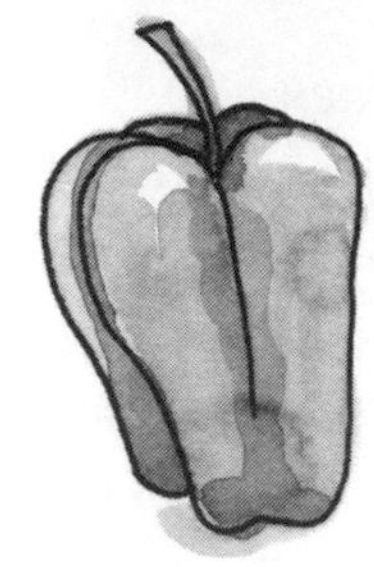

3–4 carrots, chopped
2 potatoes, chopped
3–4 celery stalks, chopped
1 teaspoon yeast extract (optional)
salt and pepper, to taste
herbs, chopped fresh or dried

Simmer all the ingredients in a pot until the vegetables are soft.

Season to taste with salt and pepper and add any herbs you fancy. I love cilantro in chicken soup!

CHANTAL'S NETTLE SOUP

My good friend Chantal started to make nettle soup after a robust patch of "volunteers" sprang up in her garden. Nettles are really good for you; they have an astoundingly high protein content and plenty of vitamin A. They also have a lovely, delicate flavor.

Nettles are best harvested in springtime when they are young, but they can be used throughout the year. Wear gloves while harvesting and handling fresh nettles to avoid getting stung—but don't worry, the sting in the leaves will cook out in the soup!

When you fancy a change, substitute kale or chard and you have yet another "superfood soup."

1 cup black-eyed peas, soaked overnight
3 cups vegetable stock, or 1 teaspoon yeast extract dissolved in 3 cups water
¼ cup olive or sunflower oil
2 onions, chopped

4 cloves garlic, chopped
3–4 cups nettles
salt and pepper

Simmer presoaked peas in a soup pot with just enough water to cover them, adding water as needed to keep them covered. It should take about 40 minutes until the peas are soft. Add vegetable stock or yeast extract.

In a separate pan, heat the oil and sauté the onions and garlic, seasoning with salt and pepper. Add vegetables to the peas and simmer for another half hour.

Add the nettles and simmer another half hour or so. Season to taste, and enjoy!

GARLIC CROUTONS

Croutons are easy and affordable to make. My kids will have soup for supper every night so long as there are croutons as well.

1 loaf day-old bread, cubed
¼ cup olive oil (add more if needed)
5–10 cloves garlic, finely chopped
chopped fresh herbs of your choice (optional)

Fill the bottom of a skillet with olive oil and place over medium heat. Add bread cubes and toss to coat. Add chopped garlic and keep tossing the bread.

The croutons are done when they are browned and crunchy. The secret to these crunchy homemade croutons is to stay present and keep stirring them!

HOW TO MAKE CLARIFIED BUTTER

Making your own clarified butter isn't difficult and is substantially cheaper than buying it from the store.

Clarified butter, or *ghee*, is made from regular butter. If you are into Indian cooking, clarified butter will enhance your dishes, as it has a richer flavor. Clarified butter can be cooked at a higher temperature than regular butter, which is one of its advantages; it also lasts longer than regular butter and doesn't need to be stored in the fridge if it's in an airtight container.

Heat unsalted butter gently in a saucepan. Spoon off the foam that forms on the surface and discard. You will see that the milk solids separate from the butterfat and lie at the bottom of the pan. Let the pan sit a few minutes off the heat. Pour the butter through a dampened cheesecloth; the butterfat will flow through and the milk solids will be left behind. Store your clarified butter in a screw-top jar either in the fridge or at room temperature.

SALADS AND SALAD DRESSINGS

BEET AND BASIL SALAD

2 big beets
4 big carrots
1 big daikon
1 bunch basil, washed and chopped
4–8 ounces feta cheese, cut into cubes or crumbled
¼ cup olive oil
3 tablespoons rice vinegar
juice of 1 lemon

Grate the raw beets, carrots, and daikon and mix with lemon juice in a large bowl. Add the chopped basil and the feta cheese.

Add olive oil and rice vinegar to taste; some people like more than others. I use ¼ cup oil and less vinegar.

This salad tastes great fresh and even better on the second day. Keep it refrigerated; the flavors improve with age. It should keep fresh for four days at least.

ANDIE'S FAVORITE LIMA BEAN RICE SALAD

This dish, adapted from a Persian recipe, is easy to make and has a distinctive, buttery flavor. You can substitute any beans you fancy in this recipe, but do try limas, as they have a light and delicate flavor.

2 cups long-grain white rice
1 cup cooked lima beans
⅓ cup chopped dill
salt to taste

Cook the rice in 4 cups of water.

Mix the beans into the cooked rice and stir in the chopped dill, seasoning with a little salt.

MACRO RICE SALAD

This is the dish that turned me on to health food when I first had it at Cranks Restaurant in London. They serve it with cottage cheese and I suggest you do, too. Make a huge amount for parties: it looks lovely and tastes even better.

2 cups cooked medium or short-grain brown rice
1 large onion, chopped
1 cup chopped parsley
¼ cup olive oil
tamari or soy sauce, to taste

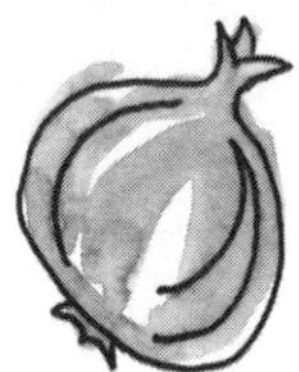

In a skillet, heat olive oil and fry onions until soft. Remove from heat and add the cooked rice to the skillet. Stir well to evenly distribute the onions.

Return to low heat and sprinkle the parsley over the mixture, stirring it in. The parsley does not need to cook; it just wilts a little. Add tamari to taste.

Serve with cottage cheese for maximum deliciousness.

COLESLAW

6 cups shredded cabbage (white, red, or green)
2 carrots, shredded or grated
⅔ cup mayonnaise
2 tablespoons vinegar (apple cider, malt, or distilled)
2 tablespoons sunflower oil
2 tablespoons sugar, or more to taste
salt and pepper, to taste
1–2 teaspoons caraway seeds

Combine shredded cabbage and carrots in a large bowl. Whisk together mayonnaise, vinegar, oil, sugar, and caraway seeds, and pour over the slaw. Mix well and season to taste. Refreshing!

DAN'S SPLENDID NOODLE SALAD

Our friend Dan is a keen surfer and self-taught gourmet. He makes a big pot of this dish for parties, and I always make a beeline for it!

12-ounce package dang myun noodles (Korean noodles made from sweet potato starch and water)
4 ounces raw beef or chicken (leave the meat out and you have the vegetarian version)
8 shiitake mushrooms (fresh or dried)
1 carrot
1 onion
2 eggs
⅓ pound spinach
3 tablespoons vegetable oil

2 tablespoons plus 1½ teaspoons sesame oil
5 tablespoons tamari or soy sauce
salt and crushed black pepper, to taste
pinch sugar
1 teaspoon sesame seeds
3 scallions, chopped
hot chili sauce, to taste

Cut beef or chicken into strips and marinate for 30 minutes in a marinade made of 2 tablespoons tamari or soy sauce, a pinch of sugar, 1 teaspoon sesame oil, and a pinch of crushed black pepper.

If you're using dried mushrooms, soak them in hot water until they rehydrate, then cut them into strips.

Blanch the spinach in boiling water for 1 minute. Drain and cool, squeezing out the excess water. Spread out the spinach and season it with ½ teaspoon sesame oil and a pinch of salt.

Scramble eggs, then cook as one flat sheet in a nonstick pan, using about 1 tablespoon vegetable oil. Sprinkle with a pinch of salt.

Cut the mushrooms, carrot, and cooked egg into thin sticks. Finely chop the onion.

Cook the noodles in boiling water until soft, 3–5 minutes. Rinse thoroughly under cold water to remove excess starch. Drain.

Cook marinated meat in a large frying pan with 2 tablespoons vegetable oil. When the meat is cooked halfway, about 5 minutes, add the mushrooms, carrots, and onions to the pan. Continue to cook until the vegetables just begin to soften and the meat is fully cooked. Remove from heat and add spinach. Allow mixture to cool for 10 minutes.

Place cooked noodles in a large pot. Add 3 tablespoons tamari or soy sauce and 2 tablespoons sesame oil, a little at a time. Using your hands or salad servers, gently toss the noodles until they are well coated with the soy sauce and sesame oil. Continue adding soy sauce and sesame oil until the noodles are well coated and seasoned to taste.

Add meat and veggie mixture, egg, and spinach, tossing again to combine. Finally, top with sesame seeds and chopped scallions. This salad can be eaten as is, or spiced up with hot chili sauce.

NEW POTATO SALAD

New potatoes are great in this salad, but don't be deterred if you only have russet potatoes. This recipe is adapted from *The Cranks Recipe Book*, my favorite cookbook! This salad goes great for holidays and picnics.

5–6 big potatoes, peeled or scrubbed (leaving the skins on enhances the nutrient value)
1 large red onion, finely chopped
handful of chopped fresh mint, parsley, or cilantro
salt and pepper

Potato Salad Dressing

juice of 1 lemon
2 tablespoons apple cider vinegar
2 teaspoons French mustard
1 tablespoon sugar
1 cup olive oil

Whisk the lemon juice, vinegar, mustard, and sugar together. Add the oil little by little.

If you are using russet potatoes, try steaming them whole in their skins to get optimum flavor. If you don't have a big steamer, you can use a wire sieve or metal colander over a large cooking pot with a lid. Steaming takes longer than boiling, but the potatoes keep their flavor well when steamed, and you can always take the skin off after steaming.

Allow potatoes to cool slightly until you can handle them. Cube potatoes and place them in a large bowl. Add the finely chopped onion. Pour the dressing on while the potatoes are still warm, and gently mix together. Add chopped fresh herbs just before serving, and season to taste.

NETTE'S CUCUMBER SALAD

Nette ran the now legendary Mamasan's Underground Bistro in San Francisco, whose dinner parties were always booked up—their Chamorro cuisine is just amazing. Nette always serves her cucumber salad with rice and chicken; it's a great side dish. Be warned: it's addictive!

1 large English ("hothouse") cucumber or 2 regular cucumbers
seasoned rice vinegar
low-sodium soy sauce or tamari
hot chili paste
1 teaspoon vegetable oil

Slice cucumbers into spears or moons.

In a bowl mix vinegar, shoyu, and oil to taste. Add cucumbers and mix well.

Allow the salad to marinade for a few hours.

EASY SALAD DRESSING

There are only two ways I can get my family to eat nutritional yeast: either sprinkled on popcorn with tamari or in this dressing. The nutritional yeast is a complete protein, rich in B vitamins, and gives the dressing such a distinctive, almost nutty flavor.

¼ cup olive oil
juice of 1 lemon or 1 tablespoon vinegar
1 dash tamari or soy sauce
1 tablespoon nutritional yeast
1 tablespoon mayonnaise
1 clove garlic, crushed
salt and pepper

Mix ingredients together well and season to taste. This makes enough for a large salad, but if you choose to make more, it will keep nicely in an airtight jar in the fridge.

AMANDA'S SALAD DRESSING

This is my other favorite dressing. It has a classic flavor, it's easy to make, and it keeps well in the fridge.

2–3 cloves garlic, crushed
⅓ cup good-quality wine vinegar or balsamic vinegar
⅔ cup good-quality olive oil
salt and pepper, to taste
1 teaspoon Dijon mustard
1 teaspoon sugar, or more
good pinch of fresh or dried herbs

Shake ingredients together in a jar. Adjust seasoning and oil/vinegar ratio to taste.

BEANS AND PULSES

Beans and pulses are an excellent source of protein. Pulses are the edible seeds of legumes such as lentils, peas, chickpeas (garbanzos), and beans. Dried beans are full of iron, potassium, and B complex while being low in fat and carbohydrates. Soak the beans and pulses overnight; the tiny red lentils don't need soaking, but all the others do. Chickpeas, kidney beans, pinto beans, black beans, haricots, and black-eyed peas can be boiled and then simmered; an hour or so should be sufficient. Add beans to soups, salads, stir-frys, or anything else!

AMELIA'S OAXACA-STYLE BEANS

My Mexican friend Amelia gave me this recipe; it is very simple but the beans always taste amazing. Amelia taught me to boil the well-rinsed beans in the water they were soaked in, which I previously thought was verboten—maybe that's why they taste so good!

2 cups soaked black beans or pinto beans, soak water reserved
8–10 cups water
pinch of salt

Bring the beans to a boil, then reduce the heat and simmer for at least an hour, or until the beans are nice and soft. Add salt to taste. And please, share the "soak water secret."

REFRIED BEANS

2 cups cooked pinto or black beans
Follow the recipe for Oaxaca-style Beans but add the following as soon as the beans have boiled:
1 tablespoon chili powder
1 tablespoon ground cumin
1 tomato, chopped
2 cloves garlic, chopped

When the beans are cooked, strain off the liquid and reserve.

Mash the beans with a potato masher and fry them in olive oil in a skillet over medium heat. Continue to mash the beans as you add the cooking liquid, little by little, using enough to get the stiff consistency that you want.

You can also cook a version with no chili or cumin. Refried beans are yummy even when very plain. I puree black beans and serve them with corn tortillas, fried plantains, sour cream, and salsa. This is Honduran style!

DEVOTEES' DAL

My friend Manmohini gave me this recipe. They serve this dal at Hare Krishna temples. The temple's free meal is a true gift economy: simple, quick, and delicious!

- 1 cup red or other lentils, washed
- 6 cups water
- 1 teaspoon turmeric
- 1 teaspoon salt
- 1–2 cups chopped raw vegetables (carrots, potatoes, celery, turnips, or others)
- 2 tablespoons ghee (clarified butter), butter, or olive oil
- 1 teaspoon cumin seeds
- 1 whole dried red pepper, broken in pieces

In a pot, mix the salt and turmeric with the cooking water. Add the lentils, bring to a boil, and cook for about half an hour, or until soft.

Add chopped veggies and simmer for another 20 minutes, or until the veggies are tender.

In a small skillet, heat the ghee, butter, or oil over medium heat. Add the cumin seeds and dried pepper; stir until the seeds darken. Pour this mixture into the lentils, stir and season to taste. Serve with rice.

REALLY GOOD RICE AND GRAINS

Rice is a versatile ingredient. I keep the rice cooker busy and offer a bowl of rice to hungry kids at all hours of the day. I keep white rice and brown rice on hand at all times. Brown rice is an excellent source of protein. Try a few different small and medium-grain varieties and figure out which you prefer. I also keep quinoa, couscous, and millet in the cupboard. They all taste different and are uniformly super healthy and affordable.

COOKING GRAINS WITHOUT A RICE COOKER

Wash uncooked grains in cold water. Boil water, add grains, and stir. Return to the boil, and reduce heat to the lowest setting. Simmer until the grains are soft and cooked. Ready to serve!

Ratios:

white rice: 1 cup to 2 cups water

brown rice: 1 cup to 2½ cups water

millet: 1 cup to 4 cups water

oats: 1 cup to 3 cups water

bulgur: 1 cup to 2 cups water

quinoa: 1 cup to 2 cups water

COUSCOUS

Boil 1¼ cups of water. Remove from heat, stir in 1 cup of couscous, cover, and let sit for 5 minutes. Fluff the couscous with a fork, and it's ready to serve.

SAVORY SPANISH RICE

This is perfect for serving with refried or whole beans, and works great inside burritos and enchiladas.

- 2 cups uncooked long-grain white rice
- ¼ cup olive oil
- 1 onion, chopped
- 2 cloves garlic, chopped
- 2 tablespoons tomato puree or 1 cup diced fresh tomato
- 3 cups vegetable stock or 1 teaspoon of yeast extract dissolved in 3 cups water
- ¼ cup chopped fresh oregano or cilantro

In a skillet, brown the rice in the olive oil for a few minutes.

Add the chopped onion and garlic and cook, stirring, until the onion and garlic have softened to transparency.

In a separate bowl, combine the stock (or water) with the tomato and any herbs you are using. Add this to the rice gradually, covering the skillet partially to prevent burns. Stir frequently until all the liquid is absorbed.

Taste the rice; if it's still a little hard, add more liquid until it is thoroughly cooked.

Season with salt, pepper, and additional herbs, to taste.

TABBOULEH

The preparation time for tabbouleh is a couple of hours, and the dish tastes best if it is left to sit for an hour or so before serving.

2 cups couscous
2 cups cold water
2 cups fresh parsley leaves, chopped finely
8–10 mint leaves, minced
4 medium tomatoes, chopped
1 cucumber, chopped
1 onion, chopped
¼ cup olive oil
juice of 1 lemon, or more
salt and pepper, to taste

Soak the couscous in the cold water for 90 minutes. Drain the water off with a sieve or by squeezing the couscous through a clean, dry cloth.

Sauté the chopped ingredients in olive oil. Stir in couscous and lemon juice to taste. Chill for an hour in the fridge before serving.

QUINOA: "THE MOTHER GRAIN"

Quinoa is an ancient grain used in South America for at least 6,000 years. It is a pseudocereal, not a real grain, as it is not derived from a grass. However, it has a very high protein value, 12–18 percent, and a delicious, delicate flavor and texture. Cook quinoa using a 1 cup of quinoa to 1½ cups of water. Bring to a boil and simmer, covered, until the water is absorbed.

I serve quinoa with steamed finely chopped kale, sautéed shiitake mushrooms, tofu cubes, and chopped scallions. You can also mix it into a green salad or a bowl of spinach leaves and add olive oil to taste. Experiment, and don't be afraid to give this to kids; they'll love it with a little tamari.

MUST-HAVE MILLET

Millet is a tiny round grain that is rich in iron, calcium, potassium, and B vitamins. Cook 1 cup of millet in 2 cups of water over medium heat. When it comes to a boil, turn the heat to low and cover, cooking until the water is absorbed. I sauté a clove or two of chopped garlic in olive oil and add to the millet. Your kids will eat the whole pan!

DISHES FOR DINNER

There are a lot of vegetarian dishes that are truly tasty and very healthy for you and all your family. Some of the dishes below are sides, and some are the main event. My family is not vegetarian, but we only buy humanely raised organic meat and poultry. In an attempt to keep our clan's carbon footprint under control, we have two meat-based meals a week. We eat fish once a week or less, and only fish that are not endangered. (For specific information, see the Sustainable Seafood guide at the website of the Monterey Bay Aquarium: www.montereybayaquarium.org.)

PRESTO PESTO

Here I share my neighbor Susan's yummy pesto recipe. Susan has a couple of luxury variations: adding smoked fish or g

2 cups fresh basil leaves
¼ cup olive oil
3 cloves garlic, peeled
½ cup pine nuts
⅓ cup Parmesan cheese
a squeeze of fresh lemon juice
salt, to taste

Roast garlic cloves and pine nuts on a baking sheet in a preheated 375°F oven for about 5 minutes.

Put all the ingredients in a food processor (or blender), and presto—PESTO!

MONICA'S SEMOLINA PIZZA CRUST

The process of making pizza dough takes a few hours, but the results are absolutely worth the effort. The recipe below makes enough dough for four large pizzas. Pizza dough keeps in the fridge for up to a week: just place the homemade dough in a lightly oiled bowl, cover it closely with a clean cloth, and then wrap it in a plastic bag.

All pizza dough should be this good! Top your pizza with tomato sauce, mozzarella, mushrooms, olives, and so forth. For a dairy-free pizza, use pesto as a topping.

2 teaspoons dry yeast or ⅔ ounce moist yeast cake
1 tablespoon honey
3 cups water
2 teaspoons sea salt
2 tablespoon olive oil
3 cups fine semolina
3 cups unbleached white flour
1 cup whole wheat pastry flour
a little semolina for sprinkling on your work surface

Heat water to 115°F. Dissolve yeast in ½ cup of the heated water with 1 drop of honey added. Set aside to rest for 10 minutes.

Pour the rest of the water into a large bowl. Mix in the honey, salt, and olive oil. Stir in 2 cups of the semolina and 1 cup of the wheat flour. Mix well, and fold in the yeast mixture, mixing thoroughly. Continue adding both flours, one cup at a time. When the dough bulks up and can no longer be stirred, place it on a well-floured surface.

Dust your hands well with flour and knead in the remaining flour—

depending on the humidity, altitude, and cycle of the moon, you may need a cup more of flour. Keep adding flour until the dough has a good, nonsticky texture.

Sprinkle your work surface with semolina and knead the dough for 2 more minutes.

Place the dough back in the bowl and brush the top with oil. Drape with a clean cloth and let rest in a warm corner for 60 to 90 minutes.

Punch down the dough and cut off a piece one-sixth to one-quarter of the ball, depending on how large your pizza pan or stone is. Roll it into a ball with your hands and pat it out into a flat circle using the side of your hand. When well flattened, lift it with your fist in the center. Stretch the dough with your knuckles, working from the center out until you have the size of your pan.

Put the dough on the pan and roll the edge. Brush with olive oil and bake at 400°F for 5 to 7 minutes, or until the crust just begins to turn golden.

Remove crust from the oven and top with your favorites, or what your favorite people are demanding! Return to the oven and bake for 15 minutes, or until the cheese just starts to brown.

This will make six medium or four large pizza crusts. You can halve the recipe or put some in the fridge for later—it keeps well for about a week. It's also perfect for catering parties!

MIKE CLANCY'S FRIED POTATOES

Mike was born and raised on a farm in County Clare, Ireland. He is a great cook, and his fried potatoes are legendary; he always cooks more than a meal's worth of spuds so he can make this dish the next day.

- leftover boiled potatoes, coarsely chopped
- 1 onion, chopped
- handful of fresh basil, cilantro, or parsley, chopped, or teaspoon of dried herbs of your choice (oregano, thyme, etc.)
- olive oil
- salt and pepper

In a skillet, heat some olive oil and add the cold boiled potatoes and the onion. Sauté, adding herbs and seasoning. Keep stirring, and remove from heat when the potatoes are nicely crunchy.

BUBBLE AND SQUEAK

leftover boiled or mashed potatoes, coarsely chopped
leftover cabbage, broccoli, or greens, coarsely chopped
leftover carrots, parsnips, turnips or other vegetables
olive oil
fresh or dried herbs of your choice
salt and pepper

In a skillet, heat some olive oil and add the potatoes and veggies; stir. Use the masher as they are heating up in the pan. Season with herbs.

Turn the heat up and add more oil if the mixture is looking too dry. Your goal is to get a nice crunchy surface on the bottom, and then turn the mixture over and get it crisp all over. Season to taste and serve.

VEGETARIAN COTTAGE PIE

4–5 potatoes, boiled and mashed
½ to 1 cup grated cheddar cheese
2 tablespoons olive oil
1 onion, chopped
2 cups textured soy protein or other meat substitute
1 cup sliced mushrooms
1–2 cups tomato sauce or chopped fresh tomato
1 cup sweet corn
1 cup diced carrots, frozen sweet corn, or both
salt and pepper, to taste
herbs of your choice

Preheat oven to 375°F.

Mash the boiled potatoes with a blob of butter, a little milk, and salt and pepper to taste and set aside.

In a skillet, heat the olive oil and sauté chopped onion until it's soft and translucent. Add the soy protein, mushrooms, tomato, and other veggies, and cook through. Season with salt, pepper, and herbs.

Transfer to an ovenproof dish, making sure to leave enough room to spread the mashed potatoes on top. Sprinkle the cheese on top and heat in the oven for 15 minutes. At the end, turn the heat to broil to get the topping crispy.

PAOLA'S BROCCOLI PASTA

My friend's mum, Paola, taught us how to make this when we were at college. She also walked us down by the Thames and picked enough rocket greens for a salad to go with it!

- cooked pasta (cook as much as you need in plenty of salted water)
- 1 head broccoli, or more, cut into spears; slice the tender part of the stalk thinly
- ¼ cup olive oil (or less, but be generous)
- 6 cloves garlic, chopped
- 1 cup grated Romano or Parmesan cheese
- salt and pepper, to taste

Steam the broccoli.

In a skillet, sauté the garlic in olive oil until light brown.

Put the freshly cooked pasta in a large bowl, and add the broccoli, garlic, and remaining olive oil. Mix well, season to taste, and serve with grated Parmesan or Romano cheese. Simply delicious!

JONAH'S FISH PIE

5–6 potatoes, boiled and mashed
1 pound white fish
1–2 cups milk
2 ounces grated cheese
handful of parsley
1 batch white cheese sauce (see Super Sauces, page 206)
2 ounces butter

Preheat oven to 350°F.

Mash the boiled potatoes with butter, a dash of milk, and salt and pepper to taste. Set aside.

In a skillet, melt a little butter and then add the fish. Cover with milk and poach gently for about 5 minutes.

Drain off the milk. (You can reserve it for making another batch of cheese sauce.)

Transfer the fish to an ovenproof dish, pour the sauce over it, and cover with the mashed potatoes. Sprinkle with cheese, place in the oven, and heat through. Turn the heat to Broil at the end if you want to make the cheese crispy.

NUT ROAST

This is a fun and easy way to add more nuts to your diet.

- 1 medium onion, chopped
- 2 ounces butter
- 8 ounces mixed nuts
- 8 ounces bread (day-old is fine)
- 1½ cups vegetable stock or 1 teaspoon of yeast extract dissolved in 1½ cups water
- herbs, to taste
- salt and pepper
- tamari

Preheat oven to 350°F.

Sauté the chopped onion in the butter until translucent.

Grind the bread and the nuts together—I prefer to leave them in large pieces, but some prefer to get the mixture really fine.

Heat the stock to a boil and add it to the nut and bread mix. Stir in the onions. Season with a pinch of herbs, salt and pepper, and a dash of tamari. The mixture should be loose.

Press the mixture into a shallow baking dish or loaf pan. Bake for half an hour.

AMANDA'S AMAZING GREENS

There is no going back to plain old steamed greens after you've tasted this. Amanda has even served her famous greens to people who thought they didn't like greens, converting many with this special recipe. Leave out the red pepper flakes if you are serving to spice-sensitive kids.

1 bunch greens (kale or chard), washed and chopped
olive oil
1–2 cloves garlic, crushed
red pepper flakes
salt and pepper
apple cider vinegar

Heat a pan over medium flame and coat the pan with olive oil.

Add the crushed garlic and red pepper flakes and fry until brown.

Add chopped greens and stir to coat with oil. Lower flame and cover pan with lid.

Stir frequently. When the greens are soft enough to your liking, add about a teaspoon or capful of apple cider vinegar and stir it in.

Season with salt and pepper, remove from heat, and serve.

HEARTY QUICHE

A quiche is a great way to use eggs in a main course. I add whatever happens to be in the kitchen for extra flavor. It could be an onion, leafy greens, or mushrooms.

5 eggs
½ cup milk
3 ounces cheese, grated
salt and pepper, to taste
1 chopped onion, sautéed, or a handful of sliced mushrooms, sautéed, some finely cut and steamed kale or chard, or anything else you fancy!
1 batch shortcrust pastry (recipe below), rolled out and pressed into a 9-inch quiche shell

Preheat oven to 375°F.

Beat eggs and milk together and season with salt and pepper. Stir in the grated cheese, adding any vegetables or other ingredients.

Pour the mixture into the unbaked pastry shell. Bake for 35 minutes, or until top is golden brown.

SHORTCRUST PASTRY

The secret to making light, fluffy pastry is not to toughen the dough with too much handling. Put your butter or shortening in the freezer and then grate it into the flour—this makes the dough easier to assemble. After mixing the dough, put it in a plastic bag in the fridge for half an hour. Then it will roll out nicely. These quantities will yield enough for a quiche shell with a little leftover for jam tarts!

2 cups all-purpose flour

1 teaspoon salt
⅔ cup butter or shortening
2 tablespoons margarine or butter
4–6 tablespoons water
1 beaten egg for sealing and glazing pies

Preheat oven to 400°F.

Mix flour and salt. Grate the butter or shortening into the flour mix. When the mixture looks like fine breadcrumbs, begin to add the water slowly. Add enough to bind the dough but not enough to make it sticky. As soon as the dough holds together, dust it with flour and chill it in the fridge for half an hour.

Roll out the dough on a floured surface.

SWEET POTATO PANCAKES

These pancakes are easy to make and very filling.

2 large sweet potatoes, peeled and grated
1 large carrot, peeled and grated
2 large potatoes, peeled and grated
2 jalapeño peppers, finely chopped (optional)
3 eggs, beaten
salt and pepper, to taste
olive oil (or other) for frying

Mix potatoes and carrots in a large mixing bowl. Pour the beaten eggs over and stir until evenly distributed. Sprinkle with salt and pepper.

Heat ¼ cup oil in a skillet over medium heat. When the oil is hot, add a tablespoon dollop of the mixture to the pan, molding and flattening it with a spatula into a burger shape. There should be room to fry several at a time. Turn them over and cook both sides well.

Drain cooked pancakes on a brown supermarket sack (cut and turned inside out).

Serve with sour cream for decadence!

PEPE STEAK

Our friend Mamasan named this recipe after her dad, who was native Chamorro from Guam. This is a quick and easy dish that is great just served with steamed rice.

6 ounces thin-cut steak, cut into narrow strips
3 ounces butter
juice of 1 lemon (or more to taste)
tamari
salt and pepper

Melt the butter in a skillet over medium-low heat. Stir in lemon juice and a dash of tamari. Add the beef, turning to coat, and cook for a minute or two. Be sure not to overcook the strips—they are much better if tender. Serve the steak over rice, and don't neglect to spoon the delicious gravy over the top—it's what makes the dish!

SUPER SAUCES

In addition to sauces, this section includes an onion gravy recipe. This is a tasty vegetarian substitute for meat gravy and works just great with mashed or roasted potatoes.

TOMATO SAUCE

3 tablespoons olive oil
1 large onion, diced
3 cloves garlic, minced
2 large carrots, minced
2 stalks celery, minced

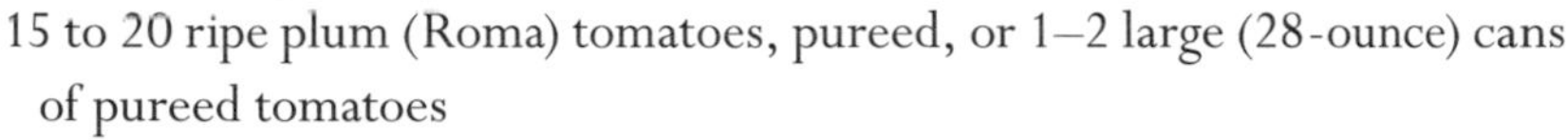

15 to 20 ripe plum (Roma) tomatoes, pureed, or 1–2 large (28-ounce) cans of pureed tomatoes
salt and pepper
fresh or dried herbs

Heat oil over medium heat and add onion. Sauté until soft. Add garlic, carrot, and celery and sauté until soft.

Add pureed tomato and bring to a soft boil. Reduce heat and simmer for about 40 minutes without a lid, or until the sauce thickens.

Season with salt, pepper, and fresh or dried herbs. Ready to serve.

WHITE CHEESE SAUCE

2 cups milk
2 ounces flour
2 ounces butter
4 ounces grated cheese
salt and pepper, to taste
½ cup chopped parsley (optional)

Melt the butter in a saucepan over medium heat, remove from heat, and stir in flour. Cook, stirring constantly, for a couple of minutes, then slowly add the milk, continuing to stir. Bring the sauce to a boil, and then simmer for a few minutes.

Season with salt and pepper, to taste. Stir in the cheese, and parsley, if you choose.

ONION GRAVY

Another classic Cranks recipe, great for serving with nut roast.

2 ounces butter
1 onion, chopped
2 cups stock (I use a teaspoon of yeast extract in 2 cups of water)
1–2 ounces flour
1 ounce cornstarch—only if the gravy needs to be thickened

Sauté the onion in the butter until soft and translucent. Add the flour and, stirring continuously for a couple of minutes, coat the onion with it. Gradually stir in the stock. The gravy should become thick as the stock is added; if it doesn't, mix a little cornstarch in water and whisk into the gravy. If you want to make this gravy smooth-textured, process in a blender; otherwise, leave it as is.

COOKIES, CAKES, AND PUDDINGS

My house rule is that if you want cookies or desserts, you have to make them yourself. This saves me from being plagued by requests for premade desserts and cookies from the supermarket. Sometimes, the kids follow through and make a batch of cookies. More often than not, they just help themselves to a piece of fruit, Mother Nature's sweets.

JAEMUS'S GINGER COOKIES

This is another of Monica's recipes; her son Jaemus calls these "the best cookies in the world." My family agrees that these cookies are indeed contenders for the title!

- ¾ cup butter
- 1 cup sugar
- 1 egg
- ¼ cup dark agave syrup
- 1 teaspoon vanilla extract
- 1 cup whole wheat pastry flour

½ cup barley flour
½ teaspoon salt
½ teaspoon baking soda
1 teaspoon cinnamon
½ teaspoon nutmeg
1 teaspoon finely grated lemon zest
1 tablespoon finely grated peeled fresh ginger root

Preheat oven to 325°F.

Cream together the butter and sugar. Add the egg, syrup, and vanilla, mixing well after each addition.

Sift together dry ingredients and add gradually to the sugar mixture; mix well. Stir in grated lemon zest and ginger.

Drop ½ teaspoon of dough per cookie onto a well-greased baking sheet. Bake at 325°F for 8 to 10 minutes. Cookies will be golden and ready when the edges begin to brown.

JAKE'S FLAPJACK COOKIES

Jake is both a great musician and a flapjack cookie connoisseur. His cookies are delicious and melt in your mouth; they're very healthy too!

2 cups oats
1 cup butter
2 tablespoons blackstrap molasses
1 banana, chopped, plus dried fruit (raisins or whatever you fancy, or leave plain)

Preheat oven to 325°F.

Melt the butter and molasses in a pan. Add the oats, banana, and dried fruit; mix well.

Press dough into a greased baking dish. Bake for 18–20 minutes.

AUSTRALIAN CAKE

My mum learned this recipe when she lived in Australia. We don't know what they call it there because her friends refused to tell her when they heard she called it Australian cake! A delicious mystery!

1 cup flour
1 cup sugar (brown or white)
2 tablespoons flaked coconut
1–2 cups mixed dried fruit
1 egg
1 ounce melted butter

Preheat oven to 325°F.

Mix all the dry ingredients. Stir in the egg and melted butter. The mixture will be quite dry, but don't add any more liquid—this is the secret of the crispness.

Press the mixture into a small, shallow ovenproof dish, and bake for about 25 minutes.

Cut into squares while still warm, then cool on a wire rack. Savor this Down Under delicacy.

SUPER-EASY SPONGE CAKE

My mum adapted this recipe by Delia Smith. She recommended it to me for birthday cake. The beauty of it is that unlike other sponge recipes there is no laborious "creaming" of the butter and sugar. You just mix everything up together. Thanks, Mum!

4 ounces self-rising flour
1 teaspoon baking powder
4 ounces soft margarine
4 ounces sugar
2 large eggs
2–3 drops vanilla extract
jam, fresh cream, and powdered sugar, for topping

Preheat oven to 325°F.

Sift the flour and baking powder into a large bowl, then add all the other ingredients. Mix until thoroughly combined. If the mixture doesn't slide off a wooden spoon easily, mix in 1–2 teaspoons of water.

Use two 7-inch cake pans, lightly greased and lined with greaseproof paper such as wax paper. Divide the mixture between the two pans and bake on the middle rack of the oven for about 30 minutes.

Cool the cakes on a wire rack. When cool, spread the cakes with jam and fresh whipped cream, putting one cake on top of the other like a sandwich. Dust the top with powdered sugar.

EASY ICING

You can add cocoa powder or lemon or orange zest for flavor to this recipe, or even a little red beet juice for a pretty pink color. Make sure your butter is nice and soft; otherwise creaming is a lot of work!

- 4 tablespoons butter
- 2 cups sifted powdered sugar
- ½ teaspoon vanilla extract
- 3 tablespoons milk

Cream the butter and sugar together. Add the vanilla extract. Stir in milk tablespoon by tablespoon until you get the desired consistency. At this point you can stir in any of the extras mentioned above.

BREAD & BUTTER PUDDING

- 8 slices of yesterday's bread (white or brown, or both; trimming the crusts off is optional)
- 2 ounces butter or margarine
- 2 tablespoons sugar
- 2 ounces mixed dried fruit (golden raisins are classic, but anything goes nicely)
- 1½ cups milk
- 1 egg
- ¼ teaspoon cinnamon
- ¼ teaspoon nutmeg

Preheat oven to 300°F.

Spread the bread with the butter or margarine and cut it into quarters.

Place in an ovenproof dish, buttered side up.

Sprinkle on the fruit, lay another layer of bread, and another layer of fruit, ending with a bread layer.

Mix the milk, egg, and spices and pour over the pudding. Bake at 300°F for half an hour. The top should be a little bit crispy.

Serve hot. Sweet and simple and extra special with a dollop of cream!

CLASSIC BLACKBERRY AND APPLE CRUMBLE

The blackberries and apples are a winning combination. You can substitute other fruit but this is a classic not to be missed. I avoid overcooking the fruit—at my house we like a little crunch!

- 2–3 apples, peeled, sliced, and cored
- 1 cup blackberries, washed
- ½ cup water with 1 teaspoon honey stirred in
- 3 ounces chilled butter
- 6 ounces flour
- 2 ounces sugar

Preheat oven to 400°F.

Fill a saucepan with a honey water, apple slices, and blackberries and gently heat for 10 minutes to soften the apple a little. Remove from heat and set aside.

Put the flour in a bowl and grate the butter into it. Chilling the butter in the freezer beforehand makes it easy to grate. Mix in the sugar.

Put the fruit in a baking dish, pouring off any excess liquid. Press the crumble mixture over the fruit and bake for 25 minutes.

Serve warm with ice cream, fresh cream, or yogurt. The most delicious dessert in late summer!

PARTY DISHES

These are the dishes I generally serve at parties; I often make a big bowl of Macro Rice Salad (recipe, page 180) and a large mixed salad, too.

HUMMUS

2 cups chickpeas
juice of 1 lemon, or more
¼ cup olive oil
1 tablespoon tahini (optional; don't be deterred if you don't have any in stock—the hummus will still taste good)
chopped garlic (optional)
chopped fresh herbs

Soak the chickpeas overnight.

Cook chickpeas in plenty of new water. When they are soft, they are done. Drain the peas and remove all the skins—they will come away easily. This takes time, but really improves the texture of your hummus.

Stir lemon juice, olive oil, and tahini (and chopped garlic if you choose) into the peas and blend or mash into a smooth paste. Add more olive oil, lemon juice, or water to get the right consistency. Add herbs such as cilantro to "dress" the hummus.

Makes a big enough bowl for a party. Serve with crackers, crudités, or pita bread. Frugal and fantastic!

VEGETARIAN SAUSAGE ROLLS

Although I came up with these pastry rolls to accommodate vegetarians, carnivores go crazy for them too.

1 batch shortcrust pastry dough (recipe, page 202)
8 ounces soy protein (the sausage formula is best)
1 egg, beaten with a little milk

Preheat oven to 350°F.

Roll out chilled pastry into a rectangle, nice and thin, as if you were going to line a pie dish with it. Instead cut the rectangle in half lengthwise so that you have two long strips of pastry.

Roll soy protein into two long, thin sausages the same length as the pastry strips, and lay a sausage on each pastry. Fold the pastry over the sausage.

Where the pastry meets, paint the surface with a pastry brush dipped in beaten egg. You can crimp the pastry joint with the tines of a fork; this will seal the roll and look fancy. Paint the top of each sausage roll with beaten egg.

Cut the rolls into 2-inch portions, and space them 1 inch apart on a lightly greased baking sheet

Bake for 10 to 15 minutes, or until pastry is golden.

HOMESTYLE SALSA

2 pounds tomatoes, chopped
2 onions, finely chopped
1 bunch cilantro, washed and trimmed
4 jalapeño peppers, seeded and chopped
¼ cup lime juice (juice of 2 limes)

When tomatoes are in season, this is a great dish to make; look for reduced-price organic tomatoes, because the better the tomatoes taste the better the salsa. Mix everything together and adjust to taste. Spice up your life!

GREAT GUACAMOLE

6 avocados
juice of 2 limes
1 batch Homestyle Salsa (recipe above)

Mash the avocados with the lime juice until smooth. Add the salsa and mix together. Healthy and pleasing.

HOMESTYLE TORTILLA CHIPS

¼ cup olive or other oil
corn tortillas, cut into quarters
brown paper bags or paper towels

In a small skillet or frying pan, heat oil. When it is hot, add tortilla pieces a few at a time and fry quickly, turning to fry both sides. Pull the chips out and drain them on the brown grocery bags or paper towels. Serve while warm with your salsa and guacamole.

SAGE'S TOMATO AND JALAPEÑO APPETIZER

My friend Sage gets hero-worshiped whenever he shows up with this dish. When I asked him for this recipe his natural modesty prevailed, and he told me that chef Brian McBride of the Blue Duck Tavern in Washington DC was the clever guy who invented it.

1 cup rice vinegar
¼ cup light brown sugar
1 teaspoon salt
1 cup extra-virgin olive oil
1 clove garlic, minced
1½ teaspoons finely grated fresh ginger
1 teaspoon mustard seeds
1 teaspoon coarsely ground black pepper
1 teaspoon ground turmeric
1 teaspoon ground cumin
pinch of cayenne pepper
6 tomatoes (1½ pounds), each cut into 8 wedges
4 scallions, white and tender green parts only, thinly sliced
2 jalapeños, thinly sliced into rings and seeded

In a medium saucepan, bring the vinegar, brown sugar, and salt to a boil, stirring. Remove from heat.

In a medium skillet, heat the oil. Add the garlic, grated ginger, mustard seeds, black pepper, turmeric, cumin, and cayenne, and cook over low heat until fragrant, about 2 minutes. Carefully pour the hot oil into the vinegar mixture.

In a large heatproof bowl, combine the tomatoes, scallions, and jalapeños.

Stir in the hot pickling liquid and let stand at room temperature for 4 hours, or refrigerate for 8 hours, before serving.

SPEEDY SNACKS

These recipes are quick to make, filling, and nutritious. Offer these rather than junk food snacks for peace of mind, and you'll save some money!

AYA'S SUPERFOOD SMOOTHIE

Aya's mom came up with this delicious and nutritious smoothie so her daughter could get "everything" at once. Aya loves it and so do we.

- 1 frozen banana
- ½ cup strawberries, sliced
- 4 tablespoons plain yogurt
- 1 tablespoon chlorophyll liquid
- 1 tablespoon hemp oil
- ½ cup orange juice
- 2 tablespoons goji berries, presoaked (optional)
- 1 packet Emergen-C, or vitamin C powder

If you are using goji berries, soak them for 2 hours before you make the smoothie.

Blend ingredients until smooth. Add a little more orange juice or water if the consistency is too thick for your taste.

KILLER QUESADILLAS

Quesadillas are so popular at our house that I wish I had a griddle and could make more than two at a time. I make these when the boys get back from school in the afternoon. It's a filling snack to hold them over during homework until suppertime.

corn or flour tortillas
grated cheddar cheese (other hard cheeses are fine too)
salsa (optional)
butter or olive oil

Heat a skillet over medium heat and add a teaspoon of butter or olive oil. Lay a tortilla in the hot oil and cover with cheese. Don't pile on too much cheese; you don't want it to ooze off the tortilla and burn on the skillet.

Add a little salsa and place another tortilla on top. Gently press down with a spatula. When the bottom tortilla is a little browned, flip the quesadilla over and brown the other side.

Lift the cooked quesadillas out of the skillet and let them cool for a few minutes before cutting into segments with a pizza wheel. For variety, add steak, chicken, or mushrooms with the cheese. Experiment with whatever you fancy!

BIG FAT SUSHI ROLLS

This is a good, filling snack—very nutritious and easy to make.

- cooked sushi rice
- sheets of nori seaweed
- any filling—strips of baked tofu, cucumber, steak, chicken, slices of avocado or carrot, or anything else you fancy
- tamari (optional)
- gosmasio (ground sesame and sea salt; optional)

Put a tablespoon of cooked sushi rice on a sheet of nori. Mold the rice into a rough rectangular shape. Place a strip of chicken, carrot, or other filling on top, and add a drop of tamari and a sprinkle of gosmasio. (Or just eat plain.) Roll up the nori like a burrito.

I make these rolls when the rice is still warm from the cooker. Munch immediately!

CHAPTER 7

Homemade Holidays

Holidays are hotly anticipated through out the year. In fact, the phrase "red letter day" originated in the old practice of inscribing holy days (holidays) in red ink on church calendars. The highlights of our family's year are holidays—birthdays, Christmas, and Halloween are our favorites. Holiday foods are often expensive specialties, but if you make your own you can afford them all! The preparations themselves become part of your family rituals, and there are hours of fun to be had making piñatas together or stringing popcorn and cranberries to make garlands for your Christmas tree.

Like many contemporary families, we have wanted to create traditions that are meaningful to us and that we can truly embrace. Throughout the year we celebrate our own festivals, as well as those from other traditions and cultures. By celebrating holidays like Chinese New Year and Hanukkah we learn about other beliefs and cultures. This is how we want our children to understand religion: that the love of God is expressed in many different ways by many different people.

I've compiled the holidays we celebrate here, gathered together by season. I hope you'll be inspired to try a few that are new to you.

SPRING HOLIDAYS

Spring festivals are among the most ancient, celebrating the returning sun and the fertility of plants and all life. Ancient henges, which mark the path of the sun at the spring equinox (the tem *equinox* comes from Latin, meaning equal day and night, 12 hours of light and 12 of darkness), remind us of our ancient heritage and our ancestors who first studied the skies.

The spring equinox is embedded in both the Jewish and Christian faiths, with the holidays Passover and Easter, respectively. Passover was initially a spring fertility festival that later evolved to become a celebration of the Hebrews' liberation from slavery in Egypt. Throughout the world the season's change at the spring equinox is celebrated, and you can incorporate foods and decorations from different cultures to make your spring holiday unique as well.

EASTER

Easter is a "moveable feast." Its date is calculated as the first Sunday after the full moon following the spring equinox. Thus the holiday falls between March 22 and April 25—at a time hopefully warm enough for you to stage a little Easter egg hunt! On the Saturday before Easter Sunday we dye eggs at our house. Friends come by with their children and we sit at the kitchen table decorating hard-boiled eggs. Dyes can be made easily, and a little artful egg dipping can produce some stunning effects. You can also paint eggs with acrylics or poster paints, draw on them with markers, or sprinkle them with glue and glitter. If you like, draw a design on your egg with a wax crayon before you dye it; the pattern will be enhanced by the dye. To get a batiklike effect, fix a sprig of a herb to the hard-boiled egg with a rubber band and immerse in the dye bath. For a tie-dye effect, wrap rubber bands around the egg any which way, leaving some shell exposed for the dye to reach.

NATURAL EGG DYE

Makes enough to dye a half dozen eggs.

- ¾ cup distilled vinegar
- 4 quarts tap water
- saucepan
- bowl
- spatula or slotted spoon
- dyestuff (use ½ head red cabbage leaves for blue, 1 teaspoon turmeric for yellow, 1 cup beets for pink, pinch of cochineal for red; for green, dye with turmeric and then overdye with red cabbage)

Hard-boil the eggs. Don't boil too many at a time—crowding leads to cracking!

Let the boiled eggs dry. You can refrigerate them until later, but dye them at room temperature.

To make the dye, add 3 tablespoons of vinegar to each quart of water and add your dyestuff. Use the proportions given above, or experiment with other dye materials. Boil for 15 minutes; remove from the heat and let cool.

Strain out the dyestuff and immerse boiled eggs in the dye bath. Let sit for 15 minutes, or longer if you want deeper colors. If you are overdyeing, let the first color dry before you immerse the egg in the second dye bath, and remember to do the lighter color first.

Remove the eggs gently with a slotted spoon or spatula, trying not to touch the surface too much to avoid smudging the color before it dries.

The delicate colors of natural dyes make these Easter eggs really special. The kids love to find the ones they made themselves, miraculously hidden by the Easter Bunny. They will peel the shells off and eat them too, much healthier than the chocolate variety!

GREEK EASTER COOKIES

At Easter time I bake Greek Easter cookies, also known as Russian tea cakes and Mexican wedding cakes. They are light, rich, and sugary—perfect with a cup of tea after a strenuous egg hunt! I make them without the toasted nuts and can vouch that they are delicious either way. Yields about 4 dozen cookies.

1 cup butter, room temperature
½ cup sifted powdered sugar
2 teaspoons pure vanilla extract
2¼ cups all-purpose flour
pinch of salt
¾ cup finely chopped toasted nuts (optional)
powdered sugar for rolling the baked cookies

Preheat oven to 400°F.

In a large bowl, cream together the butter, powdered sugar, and vanilla until light and fluffy. Gradually add the flour and salt and stir until well mixed. Add the nuts if you are using them. Form into a ball and refrigerate for 1 hour.

Pinch off pieces of dough and roll them between your palms into 1-inch balls. Place on ungreased cookie sheets and bake for 10 to 15 minutes, or until set but not brown. Remove from oven and cool slightly on wire racks.

While they are still warm, roll the cookies in powdered sugar. When they have completely cooled, roll them a second time to give them a nice, even coating of sugar. Store in an airtight container.

PASSOVER SEDER

Seder is celebrated at the beginning of Jewish Passover. It is a ritual feast with a specialized menu that tells the story of the ancient Hebrews' exodus from Egypt. Seder has a strong emphasis on children and is one of the ways that the Jewish faith is communicated to newer generations.

For the past seven years, we've been invited by our good friends to celebrate this special holiday in their home. In our friends' tradition, the Seder follows a humanist format where the story of the exodus is told and augmented by prayers for world peace and the delivery of all people from oppression. Each course is marked by the introduction of different foods, each with significance to the story. There is also a good amount of prescribed wine drinking, which translates to grape juice for the underage participants.

The kids love the *Haroset*, a confection made from apples, nuts, and wine; it symbolizes the mortar that the Hebrews built walls with when they were slaves. It is delicious served with matzo crackers. The favorite Seder moment has to be the hiding of the *Afikoman*, a piece of broken matzo which has been tucked away somewhere in the room. The child who finds it gets to match it to the original cracker and is given a little prize. We look forward to celebrating this holiday, and not just because the food is great!

HAROSET

3 apples, peeled, cored, and diced
2 tablespoons lemon juice
½ cup walnuts, chopped
½ cup raisins
¼ teaspoon ground ginger
2 tablespoons sugar
3 tablespoons grape juice

In a mixing bowl, combine the diced apples with the lemon juice, and fold in the remaining ingredients. Handle the mixture gently, but stir it well.

Chill the Haroset for at least 4 hours before serving. Serve with matzo crackers.

SUMMER

My birthday falls two days after the summer solstice, but instead of a cake, I like to make Summer Pudding to celebrate. This is a traditional English summer recipe. It takes some time and patience but is truly sublime. For me, it is the taste of summer.

SUMMER PUDDING

1 pound fresh mixed berries (strawberries, raspberries, blackberries, blueberries, redcurrants, blackcurrants)

1 cup diced fresh peaches, plums, or nectarines.

8–10 slices white bread, crusts cut off (if the bread is unsliced, slice ½ inch thick)

¼ cup sugar

3 tablespoons lemon juice

3-cup pudding basin or high-sided bowl

In a saucepan, combine berries and fruit with lemon juice and 1 tablespoon of sugar (or more, to your taste). Gently boil for a couple of minutes; the fruit should retain its shape and consistency.

Line the basin or bowl with the slices of bread, making sure they overlap. Add the lightly cooked fruit, filling the bread shell. Place a slice of bread on top as a lid and press to seal. Put a saucer or small plate on top of the pudding and weigh it down with a heavy object such as a can of food.

Put the weighted pudding basin in the fridge and chill for 24 hours. When you are ready to serve the pudding, turn the bowl upside down and the pudding will slide out. Serve with whipped cream or ice cream.

RATHA YATRA—THE FESTIVAL OF THE CHARIOTS

When my kids were young we made friends with some Krishna devotees who introduced us to their religion in an open-handed way. We loved the Krishna stories and the undogmatic nature of their faith, which celebrates the positive goodness of life, and our kids loved hearing the colorful parables of Krishna, especially "The Butter Thief," a story about Krishna being a naughty boy!

We also make a point of going to Ratha Yatra, the Hare Krishna festival that celebrates the birthday of Lord Jagannath, also known as Krishna. Ratha Yatra, the "Festival of Chariots," takes the form of a ritual procession of decorative chariots dedicated to Jagannath, his sister Subhadra, and his brother Balarama. Many devotees pull the chariots along the designated route, chanting the traditional Hare Krishna mantras until they arrive at their destination, where a great feast and entertainment awaits them. Ratha Yatra is celebrated in the West in July or August, depending on the local Krishna community. Keep your ears and eyes open for when this spectacular festival happens in your area.

Sweets are a big favorite in Hindu culture, which produces some of the most delicious candies. Here is a recipe for carrot halva. Watch out, though—it's difficult to stop eating it once you've started!

CARROT HALVA

1½ pounds carrots, grated
2 cups milk
3 tablespoons unsalted butter
¼ cup sugar
pinch of cardamom powder
toasted cashews for garnishing

Simmer milk for 20 minutes, stirring to make sure it doesn't burn.

In a skillet, melt the butter, and add the grated carrots, stirring for 5 minutes, until soft. The carrots will darken a shade.

Add the boiled milk and stir until it is absorbed. This will take about 5 minutes. Add the sugar and stir until it is absorbed.

Stir in cardamom powder. Garnish with toasted cashews.

AUTUMN

Fall is a beautiful season, and as the cold weather begins, we are compensated with our favorite holidays. Halloween is a favorite with the kids, who start planning their costumes months in advance, and pumpkin carving is a lot of fun for all the family. Don't forget to save your pumpkin seeds—just wash the pulp off and bake in the oven on a baking sheet until they look dry. Sprinkle with salt and serve while warm!

Halloween is often characterized by the candy loot from trick or treating, but there are some Halloween goodies that aren't too sugary. Try apple bobbing with your kids.

APPLE BOBBING

a few apples, one for each child
washbowl, galvanized tub, or similar vessel
water to fill the bowl

Set your bowl on a sturdy surface. The bowl should be about waist high for the "bobbers." Put two apples in the water and call your first two contestants. With their hands behind their backs, the kids try to get an apple out of the water with their teeth. The first to retrieve an apple is the winner and the prize is the apple! Don't fill the bowl to the brim with water, or you'll get a lot of water on the floor. The kids will get a little wet, so play this game after trick or treating. It should also help the kids forget about their candy for a while!

TOFFEE APPLES

6 small apples (Granny Smith or another crunchy variety is best)
1½ cups brown sugar
½ stick butter
2 tablespoons light corn syrup
2 tablespoons cider vinegar
6 wooden Popsicle sticks
pastry brush
baking sheet covered with a sheet of wax paper

Wash the apples, remove the stems, and insert the popsicle sticks in the stem ends.

In a heavy-bottomed saucepan, bring the sugar, butter, syrup, and vinegar to a boil, continuously stirring until the sugar is dissolved. Continue to cook the mixture without stirring. As sugar crystals form on the sides of the pan, wipe them away with a pastry brush dipped in cold water. If you have a candy thermometer, remove the pan from the heat when it reads 270°F. If you don't have the thermometer, lift a drop of the toffee on a teaspoon and drop into a glass of cold water; if it forms a hard droplet, remove the candy from the heat.

Holding an apple by its stick, dip it into the toffee, tilting the pan to fully cover the apple. Set the toffee-dipped apples on the baking sheet covered with wax paper. Leave them until they set, and peel them off the wax paper. You can wrap the apples in wax paper or cellophane when they are set, or serve them up right away.

THANKSGIVING

Although I didn't grow up celebrating Thanksgiving, it has become one of my favorite holidays since I moved to America. Food takes center stage at Thanksgiving, as a harvest festival, and the rich colors of seasonal produce such as apples, pumpkins, pomegranates, and persimmons make a great centerpiece for a holiday table. Try this recipe for pecan pie and you'll make your own Thanksgiving dessert affordably.

PECAN PIE

Unlike most pecan pie recipes, this filling doesn't use corn syrup; it is still lovely and sweet, though!

1 batch shortcrust pastry (recipe, page 202)

2 eggs

½ cup butter, melted
1 cup brown sugar
¼ cup white sugar
1½ tablespoons milk
1 teaspoon vanilla extract
1 cup chopped pecans

Preheat oven to 400°F. Line a greased 9-inch pie dish with shortcrust pastry.

In a bowl, beat the eggs until they are frothy; stir in the melted butter. Add the sugars and stir until dissolved. Stir in the milk, vanilla, and pecans.

Pour the pecan mixture into the unbaked pie shell and bake for 10 minutes. Reduce heat to 350°F and bake until the filling has a firm surface, about 30 minutes more. Serve warm with whipped cream or ice cream, and enjoy!

WINTER

The winter solstice, the shortest day and the longest night of the year, has been celebrated from time immemorial. Many of our Christmas rituals, such as seasonal decorations of mistletoe, holly, and ivy, predate the celebration of Jesus's birth. Christmas is the highlight of my family's winter, but we also look forward to Hanukkah, which is also celebrated in December (the exact dates move around according to the Jewish religious calendar).

HANUKKAH

Hanukkah is the "Festival of Lights," commemorating the rededication of the Temple in Jerusalem by Judah Maccabee and his brothers. Legend has it that there was only enough oil to burn a lamp for one night, but miraculously the oil lasted for eight nights! To remember the miracle, the Hanukkah tradition says that you should light one of the *hanukia* candles each night. The hanukia is a candleholder with space for nine candles (one for each night plus one candle as a "servant" to light the others).

Hanukkah celebrations also include playing Dreidel, a great little game that involves gambling for *gelt* (foil-wrapped chocolate money). Dreidels are four-sided tops that fall on one side when they are spun. Each side of the dreidel is marked with a Hebrew letter: *Nun*, meaning you get nothing, *Gimmel*, meaning you win everything on the table, *Hey*, meaning you win half of what is on the table, and *Shin*, meaning you have to add a piece to the table. The kids love this game and will play it for hours. We try to feed them latkes (potato pancakes), the traditional fare for Hanukkah, before they get tempted to eat all the gelt.

LATKES (POTATO PANCAKES)

6 large potatoes (unpeeled)
1 onion
3 eggs
⅓ cup flour
¾ cup vegetable oil
salt and pepper, to taste

Grate potatoes and onion in a colander and press out excess water. In a bowl, combine potato and onion with eggs, flour, salt, and pepper.

Heat ½ cup of vegetable oil in a skillet over medium heat. When the oil is hot, add tablespoon-size dollops of the pancake mixture. Cook on one side for 5 minutes, or until golden, then flip and fry the other side.

Remove the latkes from the skillet and drain them on brown paper bags or kitchen towels. Add more oil to the pan as you need it to fry all your pancakes.

Serve with applesauce and sour cream.

CHRISTMAS

Christmas is our favorite holiday, but when my kids were little, it became a vortex of financial worry for me. How would I pay for the presents and the celebrations? The rampant consumerist vibe that pervades our culture really got to me, and I was convinced that to celebrate successfully I had to spend a lot of money. It took a while for me to realize that I could throw great parties and give gifts that would please without spending money that I didn't have. Of course, there are always unavoidable expenditures when you are celebrating, but budgets can be brought into the realm of affordability by creating rather than buying wholesale. Making your own festive decorations and greeting cards and baking your own holiday goodies will all bring your budget into line, adding a unique touch to the way you celebrate with your family. Here are a few tips for Christmas that I've picked up over the years.

CHRISTMAS TREE DECORATIONS

We love having a real Christmas tree, and although it is an expensive item, we can offset the cost by making our own Christmas decorations. We try to look after our Christmas tree decorations, but inevitably we lose a few every year. To fill in the gaps we make chains by stringing popped corn and fresh cranberries together. Use a large sewing needle with a strong thread and alternate between popcorn and berries.

Making tiny parcels to hang on the tree can look really nice, too. Just find a little box and wrap it in scrap wrapping paper or tissue paper, add a little ribbon or glitter, and suspend it on a loop of string. I wrap up candies in little boxes so that the kids can unwrap them and eat the contents. These are cheaper and more exciting to unwrap than shop-bought, foil-wrapped chocolates. I also make gingerbread men, baked with a small hole punched out of the forehead so that they can be hung on the tree. Decorated with a little icing, these decorations look great, and they generally get eaten before they go stale.

GINGERBREAD MEN

If you want to decorate your gingerbread men with dried fruit or candy, press it into their bodies before baking. Otherwise, decorate with icing when they are cool.

12 ounces all-purpose flour
1 teaspoon baking soda
2 heaping teaspoons ground ginger
4 ounces butter
6 ounces light brown sugar
1 egg, beaten
4 tablespoons Golden Syrup, maple syrup, sorghum syrup, dark corn syrup, or honey
gingerbread man cookie cutter (or other shapes)

Preheat oven to 375°F (190°C). Lightly grease baking sheets.

Sift the flour, baking soda, and ground ginger together. Rub the butter into the mixture until it resembles breadcrumbs. Add sugar and mix well. Mix the egg and syrup together and add to the mixture; it will form a dough.

Roll out dough evenly on a floured surface to a thickness of ⅛ inch. Cut out your shapes and place them on the greased baking sheets.

Bake for 10–15 minutes, or until light brown. Leave to cool on sheets for a couple of minutes, and then transfer to a cooling rack.

MINCE PIES

Last but not least, I want to share the recipe for our seasonal favorite, mince pies. I know that everybody has a special Christmas recipe or two, and this one is mine. I have to say my mum's are still better than mine, but my pies do have a lot of Northern California fans!

Mince pies are an English specialty dating back to the Middle Ages, when they were made with meat flavored with fruits, nuts, and spices. Nowadays, mincemeat is largely a sweet and vegetarian delicacy. Some traditional recipes call for suet, but I use Rose Elliot's wonderful vegetarian mincemeat recipe.

8 ounces dried pears, finely chopped
grated rind of 1 lemon
grated rind of 1 orange
1 pound mixed dried fruit
4 ounces candied citrus peel
4 ounces glacé (candied) cherries
4 ounces dates, chopped
2 ounces slivered almonds
1 teaspoon allspice
½ teaspoon nutmeg
½ teaspoon ground ginger
4 tablespoons whiskey or other liquid

Mix all the ingredients together in a large bowl and let stand for 1 to 2 hours before using. Store in airtight jars.

Making the Pies

Make one batch of shortcrust pastry (recipe, page 202). As soon as your dough holds together, dust it with flour and chill it in the fridge for half an hour.

Preheat oven to 400°F. Grease and flour a muffin pan.

Roll out the dough on a floured surface. Using cookie cutters (or appropriately sized glasses or cups) cut out disks for the bottoms of the pies and smaller disks for the top crusts.

Place the bottom crusts in the muffin pan. Put a dollop of mincemeat in each shell, brush the pastry with a little beaten egg to seal the tops, and put on the tops, crimping the edges with a fork. Glaze the tops of the pies with a little of the egg, and prick them so that air can escape while they are baking.

Bake for 15 minutes, or until the pastry is a light, golden brown. Cool on a wire rack.

Mince pies are most delicious served still slightly warm from the oven.

HANDMADE GIFTING

Greetings cards, wrapping paper, and gift tags are expensive luxuries, so making your own, even if you aren't particularly crafty, will save money—and people will love that you put time and effort into making something for them. Save all your greeting cards, unripped wrapping paper, scraps, ribbons, and bows; everything can be reused. My friend Ariceli and I have been passing a piece of beautiful hand-blocked Japanese wrapping paper back and forth for more birthdays than I can remember!

I find it hard to throw cards away, and I keep them year after year. This provides me with a stock of great images to recycle into new cards. My basic method is to cut out the image and repaste it onto a new card and add new greetings, either by hand or simple block printing. Just as I'd choose to buy a card that a particular friend would like, I sift through the images I have for something that will work for that friend. Often I'll choose something kitschy and add some caption or speech bubble; it all depends on who I'm making a card for. If the occasion is particularly momentous, I'll spend a lot of time making something really special, usually some kind of collage with a favorite poem or excerpt inscribed.

Gift tags are easy to make, too. I'm really impressed with the tags my girlfriend Barbara makes, using a small set of printing blocks and homemade ink on disks cut from index cards. I have kept the one she made me, with my name on it—it's a small work of art! If you are going to make your own printing blocks, I think that eraser printing blocks work best for small letters. To make eraser printing blocks, carve on a clean eraser with a scalpel, cutting away the areas you don't want to print. Use ink or paint or an inkpad to print.

HOMEMADE INK

Blue ink is very easy to make using laundry bluing, which you can find at any hardware store or in the laundry detergent section of supermarkets. Put a little bluing in a glass jar and add water until you have the shade of blue that you want. Use with printing blocks made from potatoes, erasers, or some other material. Remember to seal the jar tightly and it will last indefinitely.

To make brown ink, use 4 tea bags steeped in ½ cup of boiling water. Stir in a tablespoon of cornstarch and bring to a boil while stirring to thicken the ink.

For party invites where you might have quite a few to make, replicate the same design—sometimes a simple print will work well. Potato-printing, generally considered the preserve of elementary-school art classes, is very cheap and makes unique cards and wrapping paper.

SIMPLE POTATO-PRINTING

newspaper to protect your work surface
cardstock, construction paper, or brown grocery bags to print on
small, sharp kitchen knife for carving
a few good-size potatoes
acrylic or watercolor paints
small dishes or plates for paints

Cut a potato in half and mark the cut surface with your design shape. Best results come from simple shapes; try stars, hearts, or butterflies. If you like a cutout look, carve out the inside of your shape. If you prefer a block print look, cut around the outside of your shape.

Dip your carved potato stamp into the paint, but don't use too much, and have a kitchen towel or rag to blot excess paint with. The blotting material adds texture to your print. If you use a washcloth or cheesecloth, the fabric texture will transfer to your print.

Potato prints are simple and effective. I love wrapping paper decorated in this way. The potato stamps will deteriorate quickly with use, so it's a good idea to carve a couple so that you don't have to stop printing to carve a new stamp.

If you like printing and have the time to do something fancy, you could screen-print or linocut print. These techniques need more investment in equipment and special paints, but will still cost substantially less than just buying cards.

BIRTHDAYS, ANNIVERSARIES, AND SPECIAL FAMILY DAYS

I still remember how exciting it was to have a birthday party as a child, so I try to recreate the atmosphere of those memories for my kids. I've realized that what they really want is just to have their friends all together and play all day. They have as much fun at a picnic party in the park as at any expensive "party package" event. My friends Barbara and Sage threw the best "Olympic" birthday for their son when he was 9 years old. They staged Olympic Games in the park for the kids and made sure that everybody got at least one medal. Hours of affordable and healthy fun!

All the accoutrements of birthdays and other holidays can be realized for a fraction of the cost if we spend some time in preparation. Party food, especially cakes, can swallow a large chunk of your party budget, but not if you bake your own. Homemade cakes like those presented in Chapter 6 beat store-bought every time, and decorating can be truly personalized if you do it yourself. The more healthy snacks you can make yourself, the better.

Over the years, I've refined my party budgeting to the extent that I don't worry at all about where the extra money will come from.

PARTY GAMES

Remember these old favorites? Although the piñata is the highlight of our kids' parties, the games below are much loved as well, keeping the whole throng occupied for hours.

Hunt the Thimble—Best played in one large room. Hide a thimble or other tiny object somewhere accessible for the age group. They will want to play this over and over!

Musical Statues—You'll need: a music-playing device with a pause button and age-appropriate music. While the music is playing, encourage the kids to dance wildly. When the music stops, they have to freeze, and the last child to stand still is out of the game. Continue to eliminate kids until you have one winner. I think Musical Statues is better than Musical Chairs, as it's a lot of effort to get enough chairs together in one room and somehow the kids seem to get hurt falling off chairs or hitting themselves on the wood.

Sleeping Lions—Are the partiers getting a little hot and overwrought? Play some soothing music and have the kids lie down on the floor—the idea is for them to stay as still as possible. When you see somebody moving, you can "wake" them out of the game. Sometimes they just chill out and fall asleep!

Pass the Parcel—My kids love this game. Prepare by wrapping up a small prize to start the parcel with, then wrap it with additional layers of paper. Write a series of questions or instructions and include one in each layer that you wrap. I try to make sure that the questions are engaging but not harrowing, and always age appropriate: try "Can you name five fruits?" or "Sing 'Humpty-Dumpty.' " Playing the game: Have the children sit in a circle and pass the parcel around while the music is playing. When the music stops, the child holding the parcel gets to unwrap a layer and answer the question.

PARTY DECORATIONS

My favorite party decorations are *papel picado* banners. *Papel picado* is a folk art in Mexican culture where intricate and ingenious designs are cut from tissue paper. My homemade version is much simpler but very festive all the same. The more time you have, the more detailed you can make your designs—but even the most basic cuts will make exquisite and undeniably festive party banners.

SIMPLE *PAPEL PICADO*

- scissors
- sheets of tissue paper
- string
- glue

The best size of paper for *papel picado* banners is standard letter size, 8½ by 11 inches. Place tissue paper so that the longest side is on the top. Make a fold along this top side about an inch deep and make a crease (this fold is the string fold where you will be gluing the string into place that the whole length of banners will hang from). Turn the tissue paper over so that the string fold is facing down on the table. Bring the left-hand side edge over to the right-hand side edge, folding the width of the paper in half, and make a crease down the middle. Repeat this fold two more times. Cut notches, any shape you fancy, in the folded edge. Don't cut shapes in the edge with the string fold, and remember to leave gaps between your cuts. Unfold the paper one fold at a time and cut shapes in the uncut folded edges. When you have cut shapes in all the edges, gently unfold the sheet. Repeat these steps on additional sheets of paper as many times as you need to make a banner. As you get better at cutting carefully, you can stack sheets of tissue paper and make several at once.

When you have all the sheets you need for a banner, lay them out in the order you like, leaving 1–2 inches between sheets, with the string folds all facing upward. Lay a long length of string inside the folds, connecting the sheets, and then glue down the folds with the string inside.

Make sure to use an assortment of nice brightly colored tissue papers and mix the colors up when you assemble them on the hanging string. *Papel picado* looks good inside or outside.

PIÑATAS

A piñata is fun at any celebration, especially at kids' birthday parties. When I was in school, we had a Christmas piñata tradition started by a Mexican girl named Linda; it was the highlight of our school festivities. Linda would make the piñata with a hand-picked team of helpers. She would make it strong enough for all 80 girls to get at least one turn at whacking it!

Making a piñata will take a couple of days, as the papier-mâché shell needs some time to dry. Here are Linda's piñata-making instructions:

balloon (a nice thick one is great but any will do)
newspaper for covering your work area (because piñata making is a gloopy business)
strips of newspaper about an inch wide
paste: make your own by mixing 2 cups of flour with 3 cups of water
length of sturdy string
crepe paper, construction paper, or other paper for decorating
paint or crayons
scalpel or sharp knife
scissors
individually wrapped candies, and small toys
tape

Blow up the balloon and tie it off.

Apply paste to newspaper strips, sliding off any excess paste by running the strips through your fingers. Paste the strips on the balloon, making sure they overlap.

If you have time, let one layer of papier-mâché dry before applying the next. Don't try to speed up the drying process by putting the piñata next to a radiator or in the sun, as this will cause premature cracking. If you don't have time to let each layer dry, don't worry; just try to make sure that the newspaper isn't swimming in paste. I have rarely dried each layer separately and then given it enough time to dry overall, but my piñatas have always come out fine. If you are making the piñata for little kids, a couple of layers will be more than adequate—you don't want to make it too difficult for them to smash it. For older kids or adults, do a few more layers so they have to work for their candy!

When the piñata has dried, cut a hole a couple of inches in diameter in the top with the scalpel, saving the piece you have cut out. The balloon will probably have popped already, so you can shake it out of the hole and then fill the cavity with candy and toys. Some people put little strips of newspaper in to separate the candy and stop it from all falling out in the same spot.

Make two little holes on either side of the cutout hole and thread a sturdy length of string through them. This is how you'll hang the piñata up. Now tape the piece you cut out back into place.

There are various ways to decorate a piñata—fringed crepe paper is quite traditional and pretty, but painting works just as well. If you want to get really fancy, you can stick on extra shapes; a traditional design is to add decorated paper cones. A simple round piñata can become a donkey or a dog, whatever you like, by adding a few artfully stuck on limbs. Try using paper towel tubes for legs, for example.

SIGNS OF A TRIBE

One of my favorite American traditions is the potluck party, not just because the expense is shared but also the work. *Potluck* sounds very similar to *potlatch*, the gift exchange of the Pacific Northwest indigenous peoples, but the root of the word actually dates back to 16th-century England. Travelers arriving at an inn overnight would get a potluck supper, literally whatever was left in the cooking pot, served up with bread or grains.

The potluck tradition these days occurs in churches, schools, and other community groups. Often participants are asked to bring a certain type of dish or item, to prevent the feast from consisting entirely of desserts. The basic guideline is that whatever you bring should be sufficient for a good number of the guests but not necessarily everybody. When a potluck is a small, informal affair, things tend to work out by word of mouth, so gaps in the menu become obvious and can be delegated to those who ask, "What can I bring?" I love the way everybody gets to participate in this kind of gathering, and it's a great way to be introduced to new recipes. Socially, a potluck gathering is a great icebreaker. Unlike at a restaurant, there is no pressure to leave when the eating is over. There is no limit on how large or small a potluck dinner has to be, but it is a good idea to let everybody know approximately how many people will be coming so that dishes can be sized accordingly.

Most of us really enjoy company and derive a lot of pleasure from getting together with friends. Going out and paying for entertainment is not always in the budget, so instead of staying home and feeling lonely and isolated, get creative with your social life. A simple potluck supper is an easy way to start, and creating a theme makes for more fun. One of our neighbors invited a group of friends to a potluck poetry supper, which turned out to be a load of quite drunken fun. We heard poems from Ginsberg to Hafiz, Yeats to Bukowski, and although we were all amateur readers, it wasn't at all boring. Other times we'll have potluck suppers accompanied by a Ping-Pong tournament or a backgammon challenge. Movie night is a good one if you have the kind of friends who can be quiet and watch. This isn't one that that works for us, but we often host a movie night for the kids in a separate room.

It was out of these potluck gatherings that my friends initiated their Peace Club. Horrified by the commencement of the Iraq War in 2003, they decided to stage a weekly roadside protest to advocate for peace. Six years later they are still holding the Peace Protest every Sunday morning on the main road through their village. Their community, by and large, has embraced them, and many people stop by and offer support; some bring fruit from their gardens or a canteen of coffee to share. The Sunday morning protest has become a social fixture for many people who enjoy combining activism with a social gathering. Often we potluck a post-protest lunch and then go for a dog walk. Whatever your interests, you can probably find a way to organize a social event around them. Team sports are an obvious one; getting together a five-player soccer team or a few baseball enthusiasts is generally an easy thing. Don't think people won't want to participate; we are social creatures and most people are delighted to be invited.

PIZZA FRIDAY

My husband started this fine family institution a few years ago. He was horrified at how much our pizza delivery bill was on Friday nights, especially at the end of the night when we all invariably wanted more! Initially the pizza he made wasn't the best, but after a few months he had his technique refined. We acquired a pizza stone (from a friend who rescued it from the street), which makes for a great authentic crispy crust. We started to invite friends over for Pizza Friday, and now it's a weekly fixture that we all look forward too.

If you have your own yeast starter, pizza dough is really cheap to make. The dough will be more expensive to make if you use dried yeast, but look around for premade dough in the supermarket; it's generally very affordable and cheaper than making your own dough with dried yeast. We started out buying the dough, but as our own dough-making skills improved, we gradually switched over. Making dough does take time, as you need to allow for the dough to rise. We've realized that the dough will keep nicely in the fridge in an oiled bowl, covered with a clean cloth and sealed in a plastic bag. If you make your dough a day earlier, or even earlier the same day, it will bake into a lovely crust when you are ready.

On an average Pizza Friday, we now bake seven or eight pizzas, feeding at least 15 guests very reasonably. Guests bring desserts and drinks, and our friend Don has branched out into dessert pizzas. His signature pizza is a whole wheat crust with a Nutella and fresh strawberry topping! Pizza Friday is a highlight of our week; we love the pizza and the company in equal amounts!

HOUSE PARTY!

If you love to dance and listen to music but can't afford the cover charge, it's time to throw a house party. A good party is about the atmosphere you create, and that doesn't have anything to do with money. All you really need is a sound system to play music on, and tolerant neighbors! If your place is tiny, you'll need to brainstorm who among your friends has the most party-friendly place. Organize parties as a group so you can share the preparation work (moving furniture, bringing in speakers, and so on). Remember to plan for cleanup, too. Host a Hangover Breakfast for all comers the next day.

It is rarely difficult to find somebody to be your DJ; the problem is more likely to be too many DJs. If you have a slew of candidates, figure out what kind of music they play and give them a play time. If your buddies are bashful, make up playlists and let everybody dance! Move some furniture out of your living room, roll up the rugs, adapt your lighting, and you'll be surprised at how people will get the disco vibe. Basements are good for parties, and backyards are a nice chill-out zone. Everybody brings a bottle or two, and there is generally more than enough to go around. We often make a punch or sangria, which devolves toward the end of the night into some kind of nameless witches' brew. If dancing isn't your prime objective, throw an ambient party and turn your space into a comfy chill-out room. This doesn't require rolling back the carpets, but soft lighting and plenty of cushions for everybody to flop on are a must.

HOMEMADE JALAPEÑO POPPERS

This is a perfect party snack to serve with beer. It is a little fiddly to prepare, but just make sure not to rub your eyes and you'll be fine.

10–20 fresh jalapeño peppers
8 ounces cream cheese

Preheat oven to 325°F.

Wash the jalapeños. Make a lengthwise incision in each pepper, taking care not to cut completely through. Sever the white membrane at the stalk end and scoop out the seeds with your fingers or a small spoon.

Blanch the peppers for 20 seconds in boiling water. Drop them into a bowl of cold water. Drain.

Stuff peppers with cream cheese using a teaspoon. Don't

be afraid to overstuff—any cream cheese hanging out of the incision will be fine in the oven.

Put the stuffed jalapeños in a shallow baking dish and bake for 20 minutes. Cool and serve with cold beers!

SPECIAL PARTY DRINKS

SANGRIA

I think sangria is a great party drink, especially as you can add to it during the party.

- 2 bottles red wine (merlot, cabernet, any table wine)
- 1 bottle white wine
- 2 lemons
- 2 oranges
- 2 limes
- 2 cups sugar
- 2 cups gin or triple sec (optional)
- 1 liter ginger ale or fizzy lemonade
- 2 cups fresh or frozen raspberries, strawberries, or blackberries
- 1 small can pineapple chunks or mandarin orange segments

Pour all ingredients except ginger ale/lemonade and berries into a lidded container. Chill the sangria in the fridge for 24 hours so the flavors really marinate.

Decant into a serving bowl, stir in ginger ale/lemonade and berries, and serve cold.

ALCOHOL INFUSIONS

It is not expensive to make an infused alcohol to liven up a party. Our experience has been that you don't need to buy an expensive vodka to make a tasty infusion. I generally run cheap vodka through the carbon filter of a water purifier jug and then proceed to infuse it. The general rule is 1 cup of fruit to 1 liter of alcohol. If the rind or skin of the fruit is edible, leave it on; if not, peel it off. Dice fruit and add to the alcohol in a clean earthenware, glass, or food-grade plastic container. Cover with a cloth or lid and steep at room temperature for a few days. Most fruits will be ready in a couple of days, with the notable exception of pineapple, which takes two weeks. The best way to figure out infusion specifics is to taste your concoctions; when it tastes right to you, it's ready!

Use the infused alcohol to make a special cocktail. This is a great way to offer a special drink to guests as they arrive. (I recommend pineapple vodka as a base for a fruity cocktail. One will be enough!)

HOMEMADE WINES

Homemade wines take a while to mature, but they are worth the effort and can be made without any special equipment. The only item you might not already have is a carboy or demijohn (a container fitted with an airlock).

Sandor Ellix Katz's book *Wild Fermentation* is well worth reading. He manages to demystify the fermentation process and gives some easy tips which will really help you.

DANDELION WINE

This is a family classic from my parents' neighbors Margaret and John. I copied it from Margaret's great-grandmother's handwritten recipe. I imagine her serving this to guests in the parlor at her farm in the West Country of England.

7 quarts dandelion flowers
2 lemons, juiced, rinds reserved
2 oranges, juiced, rinds reserved
2 tablespoons ground ginger
4 pounds sugar
1 gallon boiling water
dab of yeast extract
small piece of toast

Put the dandelion flowers in a crock and pour 1 gallon of boiling water over them. Let stand for five days, stirring daily. Keep the crock covered with a clean cloth to keep dust and bugs out.

Strain the liquor into a large cooking pot. Add the rinds of the lemons and oranges and the ground ginger, and simmer gently for an hour. Add the sugar and the juice of the lemons and oranges, stirring until the sugar is dissolved.

Spread a little yeast extract on a piece of toast and float it on the liquor and leave for four days to ferment.

Strain the liquor into bottles or a stone jar, and keep for at least three months.

ELDERBERRY WINE

As well as being delicious, elderberry wine can be used as a tonic and a pick-me-up. It's especially useful for colds and coughs, and I can vouch for its restorative qualities. It takes nine months and eight days to make, but it's worth the wait!

1 gallon fresh elderberries
3 pounds sugar
packet of wine yeast or baking yeast
boiling water

Wash and stem the elderberries. Put berries in an earthenware crock or food-grade plastic bucket, leaving a few inches at the top for the foam that will form. Pour boiling water over the berries, just enough to cover them. Cover the container with a clean cloth and steep the berries for three days.

Add the packet of wine yeast or baking yeast. (I use the yeast-on-toast method, using wet cake yeast or my own starter if I have it.) Stir the yeast into the berries thoroughly.

For each gallon of berries, use 3 pounds of sugar. Place the sugar in a large saucepan and add 1 cup of water for every pound of sugar. Melt the sugar over medium heat until it becomes a syrup. Cool the syrup and then add it to the berries. Leave this to ferment for five days (or until bubbling has subsided), stirring it every day, several times a day.

Strain the liquor into a carboy, demijohn, or a container fitted with an airlock, storing it for three months in a dark, temperate place—nowhere too cold, though; the wine won't like it!

Strain the liquor into another demijohn, leaving behind the "lees" (yeast residue). Leave this re-strained wine in a cool cupboard for six months, remembering to check the airlock periodically to see if you need to add more water to the lock device.

The final step is to bottle the wine. Make your own labels and be proud: you're a vintner!

CONCLUSION

Living the Good Life

My true intention with this book goes beyond how-to advice. The practical advice I offer here is not the only important component—I want to inspire you, dear reader! However many helpful hints I offer you, my real advice is an encouragement to use resources differently. I also want to instill a sense of self-reliance: the old-fashioned kind where one fixes broken appliances before throwing them into the landfill or unblocks a drain without calling for professional help.

In our grandparents' day, there was a pride and pleasure in such resourcefulness. In my case, both sets of grandparents grew all kinds of food in their gardens; I also heard tales of them raising rabbits and chickens during WWII. I remember the big basket that my grandmother would fill with potatoes from her modest garden, and I vividly remember standing in the fragrant thicket at the back of the gooseberry bushes in my father's parents' garden, sneaking a few of the sour fruits in the leafy shade. Their houses rarely changed through the years, but when something new arrived, even a tablecloth, we'd inspect and compliment it. How pretty! What beautiful quality! What a bargain! They valued their achievements and took little for granted. I aspire to the same.

Applying effort, common sense, and imagination to daily living will liberate you from a needlessly expensive lifestyle. By learning to deal with situations without resorting to spending money, you will grow your self-esteem and your bank balance.

It is always difficult to see beyond our day-to-day reality, which is generally focused on maintaining our status quo. When we do take a moment to consider the larger picture of our lives and our aspirations, we often call it *daydreaming*. Daydreaming gets a bad rap and is supposedly the territory of unambitious or unrealistic folk. I absolutely disagree! As a committed daydreamer, I recommend this form of introspection as a way to get in touch with our life's desires. No matter how unlikely our dreams may be, it is up to us to realize them. Don't spend your whole life pushing your true aspirations out of your mind—act on them!

I've emphasized the importance of career choices in this book since our culture dictates that we spend so much of our time working. Work, well paid or not, becomes drudgery when we don't enjoy it. We really owe it to ourselves to acknowledge how our work makes us feel. When talking about your job, if you hear yourself saying, "Well, it pays the bills," beware! It is important to understand that life is not a static event; things are changing all the time, ourselves included. Some people have a lifelong attachment to their occupation—my dad has never stopped loving stone carving—but this is not always the case. People often realize that they no longer enjoy their work, but the bold ones do something about it. This reminds me of my son Viv's new science teacher, Mr. Fong. He told me that he had enjoyed success in his first career, but as he got older he realized that he "wanted to give something back," and was prepared to make less money in the process. The pleasure he gets from teaching in a public school is plain to see. I hear that he is extremely strict but I also know how extremely lucky my son is to be in his classroom.

I consider success in terms of happiness, not financial rewards. Not surprisingly, I had to learn the hard way that money doesn't make you happy. The most lucrative period in my working life was also my most unhappy, precisely because I wasn't enjoying what I was doing. I had followed my interest into a career in the art world. I started a gallery and developed relationships with artists, buyers, gallerists, and critics. I loved initiating the venture and enjoyed curating shows and writing catalog copy and press releases. Little by little, the exclusivity of the art world and the absurdity of the art market got me down. Art, as a business, didn't relate to my love of art at all.

For a while, I refused to acknowledge it, arguing with myself that I'd already invested years of my energy and enthusiasm into the business and that I was making money easily. I hung on tenaciously, reluctant to give up. Luckily, my body wasn't prepared to entertain my denial and I developed a horrendous outbreak of hives, which doctors could only describe as "stress related." With my face swollen and painful and red rashes covering my body, I had to concede that my apparently successful career was the cause of my medical condition. The day I decided to change course, those pesky rashes began to diminish and I began to dream up my future. It took some time and I did some serious soul-searching, not an easy process at all. However, I knew in my heart that I didn't really have an option. Making money was all my work ended up meaning to me. It wasn't making me happy; in fact, it was making me itch like crazy!

I am inspired by my friend Penny, who always follows her dreams. When I first met her she was a video activist and a radio DJ. Her video documentaries were largely self-funded by her work as a film editor and DJ. She produced the documentary *Treesit: The Art of Resistance Story,* which her partner directed. They had no significant investors; they just ate a lot of lentils and made it happen! Penny impressed me with her happy disposition; she was doing what she wanted to do and continued to make well-received documentaries. We recently reconnected and caught up on the last 10 years. She still has her radio show but her focus had shifted from filmmaking to running an art gallery. I saw the experimental artwork she was exhibiting and asked if she was managing to make a living from the gallery. “No way!” she exclaimed. “But I started a custom picture-framing business to fund it and that’s doing really well.” I asked if she liked the custom framing business, and she did; it was so successful that she had taken on a couple of workers and taught them the trade. Penny was freed up to manage the gallery, which was exactly what she wanted to do.

At the beginning of the 21st century, many of us are aspiring to a new consciousness. Our informational technology gives us a planetary perspective that is difficult to ignore. Most glaring for me is the reality that so many people on the planet live in abject poverty while visual evidence of melting icebergs shows the devastating effects of our technology on global ecology. I believe that this is a great moment in history; collectively we have a chance to act on our knowledge and change the course of our societal trajectory. The choices we make as individuals will affect the direction that our culture takes. Our power as ethical consumers is immense: if we only buy what has been produced in an environmentally friendly way, then those production methods will grow to meet the demand.

When I realized that most commercially manufactured clothes are dyed with toxic colorants that pollute rivers, kill fish, and destroy ecosystems, I was angry and upset. Why aren’t the world’s governments legislating against these crimes against the environment? It is being left up to our grandchildren to clean up the mess! Perhaps in years to come, we will look back with disbelief at how we let these atrocities happen for the sake of commerce, but right now we need to take action. Now I only buy new clothes from companies that can vouch for their environmentally sound production. Everything else we buy is secondhand—recycling, revamping, and repairing doesn't support those unethical practices! I don't want to present myself as a holier-than-thou, self-sacrificing aesthete, but I am happy to give up supporting industries that are operating without regard for our planetary well-being.

I also want to set an example to my children, who say that the preceding generations have created a terrible mess that they have to live with. I told them that when I grew up I had no idea what was happening to global ecology, and I didn't understand the economic forces that led to poverty in the Third World. I feel it's my duty to act responsibly now, to live my ideals, and I try to do that every day as an ethical consumer.

Yesterday, I had a moment of self-doubt, wondering whether I really "walked my talk." I looked back on my day to see whether I was really practicing what I preached. I had made my kids' school lunches of healthy sandwiches, wrapped in recycled produce bags. I had poured fresh water in their water bottles. Later I sent an e-mail message to my friend Kat in London telling her that I could chat if she'd call me on her free service. (She uses a telephone company that offers the first 53 minutes of an international call free.) We talked about her redecorating—she had scored some great vibrant interior paints from Freecycle and was considering painting her kitchen wall crimson. Kat is currently rehabilitating herself after a bad car accident by attending a free yoga class and a free Qi Gong class every week. The only cost is bus fare. She is making beautiful quilts out of recycled fabrics, so I told her about a cool DIY craft website (etsy.com) where artisans display and sell their work without paying any fees. My phone is wireless, so I was able to prune back the rambling blackberry bushes as we chatted. I picked enough berries for a pie, then weeded my vegetable patch, and harvested a bowl of tiny new potatoes.

Later, I made Aya's Superfood Smoothie (recipe, page 217) for my husband, who was feeling pale and depleted after working long hours in his basement studio. I also made a lentil stew for dinner using what we had on hand in the cupboard: a cup of lentils, an onion, two carrots, two potatoes (one white, one sweet), a teaspoon of yeast extract, and a sprig of oregano from the garden. I cooked a cup of quinoa in the rice cooker and I made a skillet full of garlic croutons with olive oil, a few stray cloves of garlic, and yesterday's ciabatta bread. I also worked on my manuscript, walked my dog, drove to soccer practice, and treated myself to half an hour in my favorite thrift store. There I found a beautiful hardback copy of *The Great Gatsby* for 99 cents. I bought it with one of the $3 coupons that they give if you bring in a donation. I am going to do a little DIY decoupage on the cover and give it to a friend for his birthday. *Gatsby* is his favorite novel, and I think he will love this copy.

When I had recapped my day, I felt better. I'd had a full, productive day, crossed a few things off my to-do list, and I hadn't resorted to any unnecessary expenditures. It was a useful exercise to scrutinize my day, if only for peace of mind. I lived by my "fix it, make it, grow it, bake it" philosophy and brought happiness to my loved ones and community. I keep on trying to utilize my time and resources the best I can. I remind myself of the seventh generation philosophy from the Great Law of the Iroquois Confederacy: "In our every deliberation, we must consider the impact of our decisions on the next seven generations." This wisdom is essential for the future health and happiness of our children, and our planet depends upon it.

Perfection is always beyond us, but striving for the best daily realization of life on earth is good enough for me. I wish you much luck and courage in creating your own good life!

BIBLIOGRAPHY

Bay Laurel, Alicia. *Living on the Earth: Celebrations, Storm Warnings, Formulas, Recipes, Rumors, and Country Dances Harvested by Alicia Bay Laurel*. New York: Random House, 1971.

Boots, Gypsy. *Bare Feet and Good Things to Eat*. Los Angeles: Virg Nover Printers, 1965.

Brand, Stewart. *Whole Earth Catalog*. Portola Institute, 1970.

Cantor, David, Kay Cantor, and Daphne Swann. *The Cranks Recipe Book*. M. Dent & Sons, 1982.

Carson, Rachel. *Silent Spring*. Boston: Houghton Mifflin, 1962.

Dass, Ram. *The Only Dance There Is*. New York: Anchor Press/Doubleday, 1974.

Dustman, Karen Dale. *The Women's Fix-It Book: Incredibly Simple Weekend Projects & Everyday Home Repair*. Chandler House Press, 1998.

Emery, Carla. *The Encyclopedia of Country Living*. 10th edition. Seattle: Sasquatch Books, 1994

Elgin, Duane. *Promise Ahead: A Vision of Hope and Action for Humanity's Future*. New York: Harper Paperbacks, 2001.

Elliot, Rose. *Rose Elliot's Vegetarian Kitchen*. HarperCollins, 1999.

Fisher, Robert. *Contact and Conflict: European Relations in British Columbia 1774–1890*. University of British Columbia Press, 1977.

Fuller, Buckminster. *Operating Manual for Spaceship Earth*. Southern Illinois University Press, 1969.

Katz, Sandor Ellix. *Wild Fermentation*. Chelsea Green Publishing Co., 2003.

Knight, Brenda. *Rituals for Life: Create Your Own Sacred Ceremonies*. F & W Publications, 2004.

Kushi, Michio. *The Book of Macrobiotics: The Universal Way of Health and*

Happiness. Tokyo: Japan Publications, 1977.

McKenna, Terence. *Food of the Gods: The Search for the Original Tree of Knowledge*. New York: Bantam Books, 1992.

McLuhan, Marshall. *Understanding Media: The Extensions of Man*. New York: Mass Market Paperbacks, 1964.

Mnimh, Penelope Ody. *Medicinal Herbs*. London: Dorling Kindersley, 1997.

Wormwood, Valerie. *The Fragrant Pharmacy: A Home and Health Guide to Aromatherapy and Essential Oils*. Macmillan London, 1990.

ONLINE SOURCES

American Community Gardening Association *(www.communitygarden.org)*

Authorama (*www.authorama.com*)

Babel Nation (*www.babelnation.com*)

By Gosh (*www.bygosh.com*)

CouchSurfing (*www.couchsurfing.com*)

The Diggers (*www.diggers.org*)

Eden Workshops (*www.edenworkshops.com*)

eHow (*www.ehow.com*)

Energy Star *(www.energystar.gov)*

Free Farm Stand (*www.freefarmstand.org*)

Farm To School (*www.farmtoschool.org*)

Freecycle *(www.freecycle.org)*

Freegans *(www.freegan.info)*

Free Online Games (*www.freeonlinegames.com*)

Free Games (*www.games.com*)

Gazelle (*www.gazelle.com*)

Greenfeet.net *(Chadderdon article: www.greenfeet.net/newsletter/whatsinpaint.shtml)*

Green Home Guide *(Pennock article: http://greenhomeguide.com/know-how/article/selecting-green-paint)*

How Stuff Works (*www.howstuffworks.com*)

Hulu (*www.hulu.com*)

Instructables (*www.instructables.com*)

Laura Cornell Yoga *(www.lauracornell.com)*

Livemocha (*www.livemocha.com*)

Magic Keys (*www.magickeys.com*)

ManyBooks (*www.manybooks.net*)

Meat Free Mondays (*www.meatfreemondays.co.uk*)

Metacafe (*www.metacafe.com*)

Milliande (*www.milliande.com*)

My Footprint (*www.myfootprint.com*)

My Theater (*www.mytheater.com*)

Nike Reuse a Shoe (*www.nikereuseashoe.com*)

Permaculture San Francisco *(www.permaculture-sf.org)*

Pogo (*www.pogo.com*)

Project Gutenberg (*www.gutenberg.org*)

Questia *(www.questia.com)*

Really Really Free Market (*www.reallyreallyfree.org*)

REOH *(Resources for Environmental and Occupational Health: www.reoh.com)*

Scrap (*www.scrap-sf.org*)

Servas (*www.servas.org*)

SF Glean (*www.sfglean.org*)

wikiHow (*www.wikihow.com*)

ABOUT THE AUTHOR

Photo by: Barbara Renaud Bray

BILLEE SHARP was a contemporary art curator and gallerist in London, working with the YBA group of artists, before moving to America in 1993. She took up residence in San Francisco, where she started a family, ran an independent record label, founded a green cleaning business, curated many multimedia cultural events, and cofounded the Mission Casbah, an artisan crafts market.